Miniatures from the Heart
Judges' Choice

by Joanne Nolt

CHITRA PUBLICATIONS

Copyright ©1995 Chitra Publications

All Rights Reserved. Published in the United States of America.

Chitra Publications
2 Public Avenue
Montrose, Pennsylvania 18801

No part of this publication may be reproduced or transmitted in any form or by any means, electronic or mechanical, including photocopy, recording, or any information storage and retrieval system now known or to be invented, without permission in writing from the publisher, except by a reviewer who wishes to quote brief passages in connection with a review written for inclusion in a magazine, newspaper, or broadcast.

First Printing: 1995

Library of Congress Cataloging-in-Publication Data

Nolt, Joanne S., 1948-
    Miniatures from the heart: judge's choice/Joanne S. Nolt,
Pamela Moss Watts.
      p. cm.
  ISBN 1-885588-00-3
  1. Quilting—Patterns. 2. Miniature quilts. I. Watts, Pamela
II. Title.
TT835.N64 1994
746.46'0228—dc20
                                              94-45253
                                                 CIP

Editor: Joanne S. Nolt
Design and Illustrations: Pamela Moss Watts
Photographs: Stephen J. Appel Photography, Vestal, New York

Special thanks to Angela Simic, owner of The Pelican in Endwell, New York, for letting us photograph our quilts in her quaint, little shop.

Introduction

The 1993 Miniatures from the Heart Contest is long past, but we just had to share more of the excitement of its 500 wonderful quilts. In addition to the prizewinners (which can be found in Issue #13 of Miniature Quilts magazine), we selected 21 other contest quilts we knew you'd admire and want to make. They're all in here—from quick and easy patterns like "Stacked Bricks" and "Antiquated Nine Patch" to more challenging ones like "Hunter's Star." If you love to appliqué, you'll love the darling "Gobble, Gobble, Gobble" quilt.

Is piecing your favorite part of quiltmaking? Whether you prefer sewing by hand or machine, you'll find patterns that seem to call your name! Start with the tried-and-true methods you know or stretch yourself a bit and tackle a new quiltmaking technique. It was a pleasure to write the patterns for these terrific quilts. As I worked, I envisioned the ways I'd use my fabrics in them! Now the book is finished and I can start stitching! Join me, won't you?

Joanne

Contents

Mini Stitching Tips 5

Patterns

Log Cabin 6
My Amish Bars & Vines 7
March Madness 8
Honey, I Shrunk the Quilt! 9
Gobble, Gobble, Gobble 10
Boston "T" Party 12
Cabins, Hearts and Scraps 13
Soaring About America 14
Old Tyme Puzzle 16
A Wrench in the Works 17
Hunter's Star 24
Spools Everywhere 25
Star Tricks 26
Quilter's Dream 28
Antiquated Nine-Patch 29
Autumn Engagement 30
Silk Memories 32
Windblown Lily 34
Magnolia 36
Stacked Bricks 37
Raspberry Confetti 38

Photo Gallery 18-23

Patterns in this book are rated for level of difficulty as follows:

Beginner   Intermediate   Advanced

Mini Stitching Tips

Fabric Selection

We recommend 100% cotton for most projects because it is easy to finger press and handles nicely. The yardage requirements in our patterns are based on a standard 44" wide bolt. However, many of the quilts can be made from a healthy scrap bag.

Fabric Preparation

We suggest washing your fabrics before using them in your minis. Make sure that you test all of your fabrics to be sure they are colorfast.

Templates

Trace pattern pieces on clear plastic. Use a permanent marker to mark the name of the block, total number of pieces, pattern letter and grainline on each template.

Pieced Patterns

Our patterns include 1/4" seam allowances unless otherwise noted. The solid line is the cutting line and the dashed line is the sewing line. For hand piecing, make the template without the seam allowance; for machine piecing, include the seam allowance.

Appliqué Patterns

A seam allowance is not included on appliqué pieces. The solid line is the sewing line. Make a template and trace around it on the right side of the fabric. Then "eyeball" a 1/8" to 1/4" seam allowance when cutting the fabric. Clip *inside* curves almost to the pencil line, so they will turn under smoothly.

Marking Fabric

We recommend Berol® Verithin® pencils for dark fabrics, red Verithin or No. 2 pencil for light fabrics. Always use a sharp pencil and a light touch. Lay a piece of fine-grained sandpaper under the fabric to keep it from slipping while you mark it.

Hand Sewing

Because the seams are short, use a thin, short appliqué needle ("sharp") to ensure a flat seam with no holes. Sew on the marked sewing line only. Trim pieced seams to 1/8" to reduce bulk at intersections.

Machine Sewing

Set stitch length to 14 stitches per inch. Blanche Young shares this tip for making a stitching guide on your sewing machine. Place a clear plastic ruler under the needle, to the left side, and align the right edge of the ruler 1/4" from the point of the needle and along the throat plate. Cut a length of Moleskin foot pad about 1/4" x 2" and stick it in place at the ruler's edge. Feed fabric under the needle, touching this guide.

Pressing

Press seams toward the darker of the two fabrics. Press abutting seams in opposite directions whenever possible. Use a dry iron and press carefully. Little blocks are easy to distort.

Mitering Corners

Center each border strip on a side so the ends extend equally and sew, leaving 1/4" unstitched at the beginning and end of the stitching line. Do not stitch into the seam allowance.

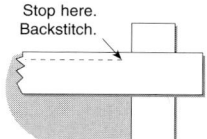

On the ironing board, smooth the border strips out for one corner and lay one extension over the other. Fold the top extension under at a 45° angle so the end is aligned with the strip below. Press a crease to mark the angle. Pin the ends together in several places.

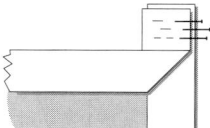

Fold the quilt on the diagonal, right sides together, and sew on the crease, starting at the seamline and running off the outer edge. Open the corner and check to see that it lies flat before trimming away excess fabric. Repeat for the remaining corners.

Making Bias Strips

Most miniature work requires bias strips of less than 25". Begin with an 18" fabric square. Lay your clear plastic ruler diagonally across the square and cut from corner to corner. Cut a bias strip the width you require measuring from the diagonal cut. This strip will be 25". Additional diagonal cuts will decrease in length. Cut as many as required for your pattern.

Finishing the Quilt

Batting and Quilting

Use a low-loft or very thin batting. Some quilters peel batting into two layers (leaving some loft and good drape), others use flannel as a filler. Layer the quilt sandwich as follows: backing, wrong side up; batting; quilt top, right side up. Baste or pin the layers together. Very small quilts can be lap-quilted without a hoop. Larger pieces can be quilted in a hoop or small frame. Use a short, thin needle ("between") and small stitches that will be in scale with the little quilt. Thread the needle with a single strand of quilting thread and knot the thread. Insert the needle through the quilt top and batting (not the backing) an inch away from where you want to begin quilting. Gently pull the thread to pop the knot through the top and bury it in the batting.

Cut simple designs from clear plastic adhesive-backed shelf paper. They'll stick and re-stick long enough to finish the quilt. Use masking tape to mark grids. Remove the tape when you're not quilting to avoid leaving a sticky residue. Mark judiciously with pencils; thick lines that won't go away really stand out on a small quilt. Our experience is that too much quilting can flatten a miniature and set the quilt "out of square." Too much puffiness can detract from the scale of the quilt. Experiment and decide what you like best. When the quilting is finished, trim the back and batting even with the top.

Binding

For most quilts, a double-fold French binding is an attractive, durable and easy finish. To make 1/4" finished binding, cut each strip 1 3/4" wide on the crossgrain of the fabric. Sew binding strips together with diagonal seams; trim and press seams open.

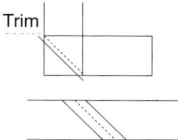

Fold the binding strip in half lengthwise, wrong sides together and press. Position the binding strip on the right side of the quilt top, so that all raw edges are even. Leave approximately 4" of the binding strip free. Beginning several inches from one corner, stitch the binding to the quilt with a 1/4" seam allowance. When you reach a corner, stop the stitching line exactly 1/4" from the edge of the quilt. Backstitch, clip threads and remove the quilt from the machine. Fold the binding up and away, creating a 45° angle, as shown.

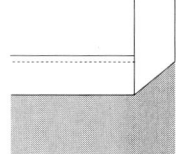

Fold the binding down as shown, and begin stitching at the quilt edge through all layers.

Continue stitching around the quilt in this manner. To finish the binding, overlap the binding strips at the starting point the width of the strip (1 3/4"). Stitch the binding ends right sides together with a diagonal seam. Lay the binding flat and finish stitching. Clip the corners and fold the binding over the edges of the quilt to the back. Blindstitch it to the back of the quilt covering the stitches.

Sign Your Quilt

Small quilts are revered by collectors, and the little quilts we make today will be treasured by our families and friends. On muslin, using embroidery, cross-stitch or permanent marker, write your name and other important data like your city, the date the quilt was completed and who the quilt was made for and attach it to the back of the quilt. Someone will be glad you did!

Barn Raising

Straight Furrows

Sunshine and Shadow

Shown on page 18

Log Cabin
An old-fashioned favorite!

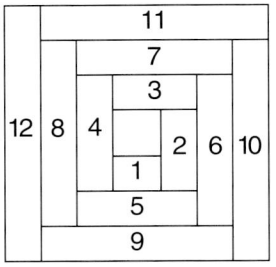

Full-Size Block

QUILT SIZE 8 3/4" x 11 1/2"
BLOCK SIZE 1 3/8"

MATERIALS

Yardage is estimated for 44" fabric.
- Scraps of 4 different darks and 3 different lights
- Permanent marker
- 5" square of clear template plastic
- 11" x 14" piece of batting
- 11" x 14" piece of backing fabric

PREPARATION

- Trace pieces A-H onto template plastic and cut out. Mark the pattern letter on each template with permanent marker.

CUTTING

Pattern pieces are full size and do not include a seam allowance. Trace the templates on the fabric leaving 1/2" between them. Cut out each piece adding 1/4" seam allowance. This will make the pieces easier to handle. Trim the seams to a scant 1/8" after stitching.

For each of 48 blocks:
- Cut 1: A, dark center
- Cut 1: B, first light, position 1
- Cut 1: C, first light, position 2
- Cut 1: C, first dark, position 3
- Cut 1: D, first dark, position 4
- Cut 1: D, second light, position 5
- Cut 1: E, second light, position 6
- Cut 1: E, second dark, position 7
- Cut 1: F, second dark, position 8
- Cut 1: F, third light, position 9
- Cut 1: G, third light, position 10
- Cut 1: G, third dark, position 11
- Cut 1: H, third dark, position 12

Also:
- Cut 1: 1 3/4" x 44" strip, second dark, for the binding

DIRECTIONS

- Use a thin appliqué needle ("sharp"). Sew on the marked line only. Trim seams to 1/8" to reduce bulk.
- Stitch the center square, A, to the first light B right sides together. Use the stitching line as your guide. Finger press the seam open.
- Stitch first light C at position 2. Lay the fabrics right side together and stick a straight pin through the fabric at the beginning and end of the seamline.
- Once the seamlines are lined up rearrange the pins for stitching. Stitch the seam.
- Proceed around the square in numerical order, utilizing the techniques above. Trim and finger press each seam. Complete all 48 blocks.
- Lay out the completed blocks in 8 rows of 6 in the Barn Raising pattern or any other Log Cabin design, like the ones shown at left.
- Stitch the blocks into rows. Join the rows.
- Finish according to *Mini Stitching Tips*, using a continuous binding.

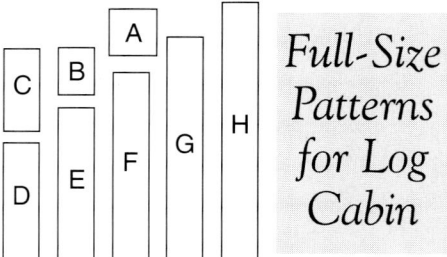

Full-Size Patterns for Log Cabin

My Amish Bars & Vines

Shown on page 18

Strip piecing makes this mini go fast!

QUILT SIZE 9 3/8" x 12 1/2"

MATERIALS

Yardage is estimated for 44" fabric.
- 2" x 18" strip of 9 bright solids
- 18" square of black for sashing and border
- 12" x 13 1/2" piece of backing fabric
- 12" x 13 1/2" piece of batting
- Contrasting silk thread
- Chalk marker

CUTTING

Dimensions include 1/4" seam allowance.
- Cut 1: 7/8" x 18" strip, from each of the 9 solids
- Cut 4: 1 3/8" x 8 3/4" strips, black
- Cut 2: 1 3/8" x 7 3/8" strips, black
- Cut 2: 1 1/2" x 11" strips, black
- Cut 2: 1 1/2" x 9 7/8" strips, black

DIRECTIONS
- Stitch the nine 7/8" x 18" strips together along their long sides, in any order you choose.
- Cut eight 1 5/8" slices from the pieced strip.

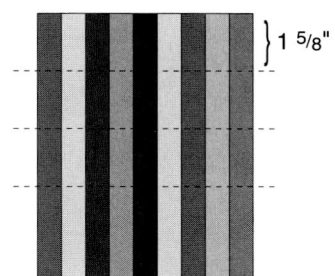

- Stitch 3 slices together end to end, creating a pieced row of 27 bars. Remove (unsew) 5 bars from one end, as shown.

- Make 2 more pieced rows each with a total of 27 bars. Remove 5 bars from each of the pieced rows. You can remove bars from either or both ends to give the quilt a scrappier look, as long as there are 22 bars in the finished pieced row.
- Lay out the 3 pieced rows and four 1 3/8" x 8 3/4" black strips alternating the strips and rows, as shown. Stitch them together.

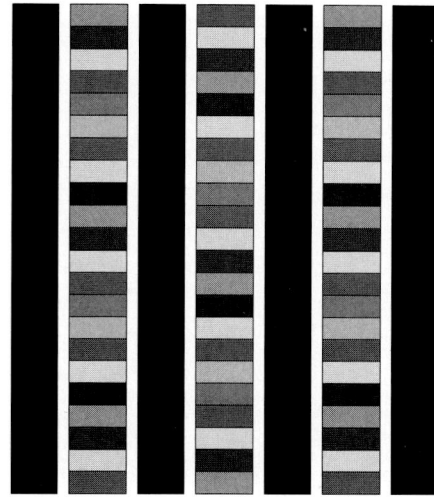

- Stitch the 1 3/8" x 7 3/8" black strips to the top and bottom of the quilt.
- Using 3/4"-wide fabric strips in a variety of colors and lengths make 2 middle border strips measuring 3/4" x 10 1/2" and stitch them to the long sides of the quilt. Refer to the photo as necessary.
- In the same manner, make 2 more pieced strips with a finished measurement of 3/4" x 7 7/8". Stitch a pieced strip to each remaining side of the quilt.
- Stitch the 1 1/2" x 11" black strips to the long sides of the quilt.
- Stitch the 1 1/2" x 9 7/8" strips to the remaining sides of the quilt.
- Draw a vine in chalk around the first black border and on the black strips between the pieced rows. Use a running

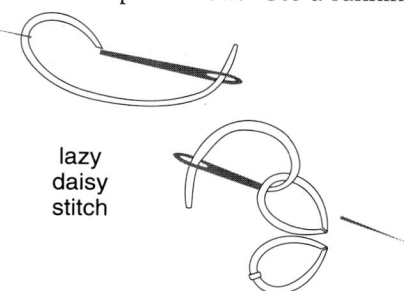

lazy daisy stitch

stitch in silk thread to stitch the vine over the chalk placement line. Add a lazy daisy stitch at intervals around the vine.
- Embroider a running stitch in silk thread in the outer border 1/4" from the pieced border.
- Layer the back and top right sides together. Lay the batting on the bottom. Trim the back and batting even with the top. Treating these 3 layers as a single unit, stitch around the outside 1/4" from the raw edge. Leave 5" unstitched.
- Trim the batting close to the stitching.
- Turn the quilt right side out.
- Stitch the opening closed using tiny hidden stitches.

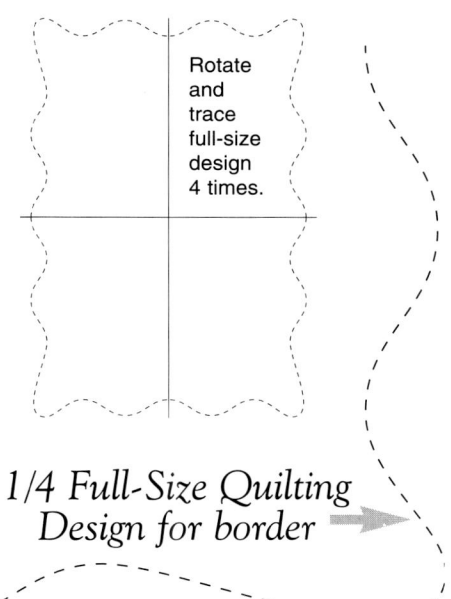

Rotate and trace full-size design 4 times.

1/4 Full-Size Quilting Design for border

Shown on page 18

March Madness
You'll be mad about this beauty!

QUILT SIZE 23 1/2" square
BLOCK SIZE 4 1/2" square

MATERIALS
Yardage is estimated for 44" fabric.
- 5" square of 64 different basket fabrics
- 3/4 yard light, for the background and border
- 1/8 yard dark, for the binding
- 26" square of backing fabric
- 26" square of batting
- 5" square of clear plastic template

CUTTING
For each of 64 basket fabrics:
- Cut 1: 5/8" x 2" bias strip (use a 2 1/2" square)
- Cut 1: A
- Cut 2: B

Also:
- Cut 16: 2 5/8" squares, light
- Cut 64: 1 1/4" x 2" rectangles, light
- Cut 32: 2 3/8" squares, light, in half diagonally, or cut 64 A's
- Cut 2: 3" x 18 1/2" strips, light
- Cut 2: 3" x 23 1/2" strips, light
- Cut 3: 1 3/4" x 44" strips, dark, for the binding

PREPARATION
- Lay the 2 5/8" light squares over the full-size pattern. Hold the fabric and pattern to a light source such as a window or light box. Trace the placement for the basket handles on each square.

DIRECTIONS
- Fold one long side of the 5/8" x 2" bias strip over 1/3 of the strip wrong sides together and press to hold the fold. Trim to a scant 1/8".
- Examine the photo of the quilt. Each basket (and its handle) is a different color. Choose fabrics now in groups of 4 for each block.
- Appliqué the folded side of each bias strip to the inside curve of the handle using the drawn lines as a guide.
- Use your needle to turn under the remaining side. Let the ends extend into the seam allowance. When the A is attached the ends will be sewn down.
- Stitch an A to each side of a 2 5/8" light square, as shown. Sew opposite sides first. Match the color A to the handle color. Use all the A's making 16 block centers.

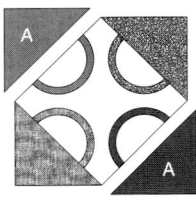

- For each block center lay out the 2 matching B's for each basket. Place a 1 1/4" x 2" light rectangle between the B's.

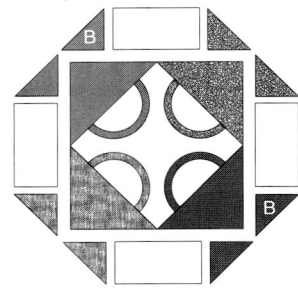

- Stitch a B to each end of a 1 1/4" x 2" light rectangle. Remember you are sewing different color B's to the same rectangle. Replace each section in the layout as you proceed around the block.
- Stitch the B/rectangle units to the appropriate side of the center section.
- Stitch a light A to each block corner, squaring the block.

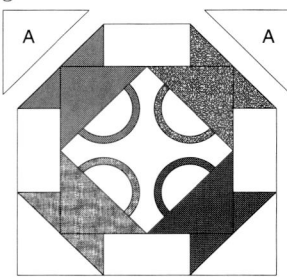

- Stitch the blocks into 4 rows of 4. Join the rows.
- Stitch the 3" x 18 1/2" light strips to opposite sides of the quilt.
- Stitch the 3" x 23 1/2" light strips to the remaining sides of the quilt.
- Finish as described in *Mini Stitching Tips* using the 1 3/4" strips in a continuous binding.

Full-Size Patterns for March Madness

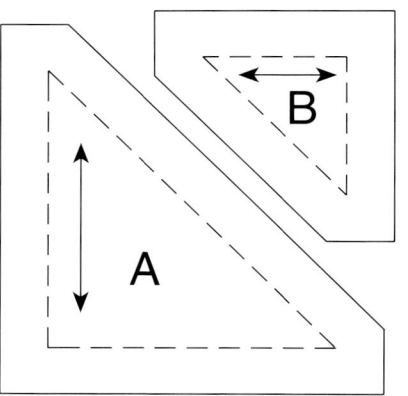
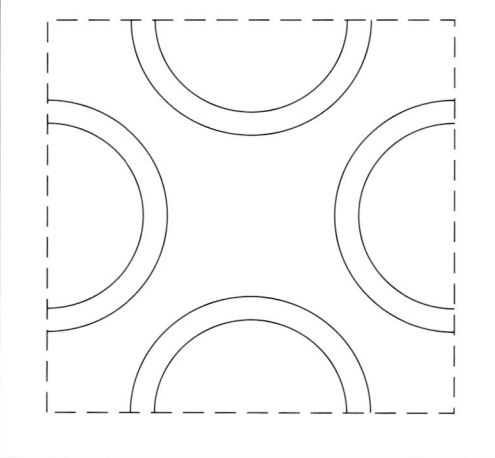

Honey, I Shrunk the Quilt!

Shown on page 18

A treasure in any size!

QUILT SIZE 18 1/2" square
BLOCK SIZE 2 1/2" square

MATERIALS

Yardage is estimated for 44" fabric.
- 5" square of blue for each of 41 blocks
- 3/4 yard of white
- 1/2 yard of gray for the sashing and border
- 21" square of backing fabric
- 21" square of batting

CUTTING

Dimensions include 1/4" seam allowance.

Blue for each of 25 blocks:
- Cut 2: 1 7/8" squares in half diagonally or cut 4 A's
- Cut 1: 1" x 4 1/2" strip

Blue for each of 12 half blocks:
- Cut 1: A
- Cut 2: B
- Cut 1: 1" x 2 1/2" rectangle

Blue for each 4 corner blocks:
- Cut 2: B
- Cut 1: 1" square

Also:
- Cut 25: 1" x 4 1/2" strips, white
- Cut 56: 1 7/8" squares, white, in half diagonally or cut 112 A's
- Cut 12: 1" x 2 1/2" rectangles, white
- Cut 3: 2" squares, white, in quarters diagonally or cut 12 C's
- Cut 4: D, white
- Cut 8: 2 1/4" squares, white, in quarters diagonally or cut 32 B's
- Cut 2: 1 3/4" x 44" strips, white, for the binding
- Cut 69: 1" squares, white
- Cut 64: 1" x 3" strips, gray, for the sashing
- Cut 2: 1" x 17 1/2" strips, gray for the border
- Cut 2: 1" x 18 1/2" strips, gray for the border

DIRECTIONS

For each block:
- Stitch a 1" x 4 1/2" blue strip to a 1" x 4 1/2" white strip right sides together along their length.
- Cut four 1" slices from the pieced strip.

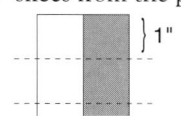

- Stitch a blue A to a white A, forming a pieced square, Make 4 pieced squares.

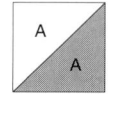

- Lay out a block using the 4 slices, 4 pieced squares and 1" white square.

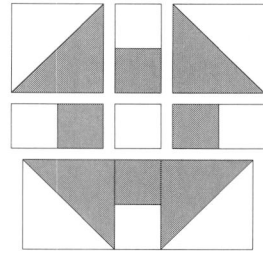

- Stitch the pieces into 3 rows. Join the rows. Complete 25 blocks.

For each half block:
- Stitch a blue A to a white A forming a pieced square.
- Stitch a 1" x 2 1/2" white rectangle to a 1" x 2 1/2" blue rectangle along their length.
- Cut two 1" slices from the pieced strip.

(continued)

Assembly Diagram

Full-Size Patterns for Honey, I Shrunk the Quilt!

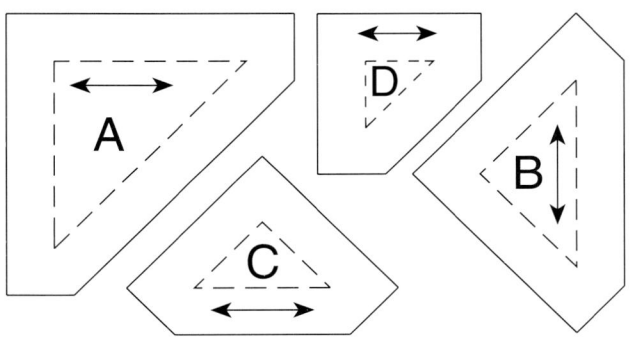

Honey, I Shrunk the Quilt!
(continued)

- Stitch a blue B to a white B, as shown. Make a second pieced triangle reversing the colors.

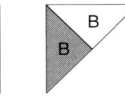

- Lay out a half block using the 2 slices, a pieced square, the 2 B triangles and a white C triangle, as shown.

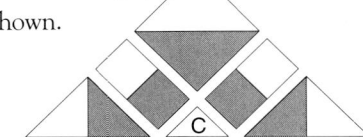

- Stitch the pieces into rows. Join the rows. Make 12.

For each corner block:
- Stitch a white B to a blue B. Make a second pieced triangle reversing the colors.
- Stitch a 1" white square to a 1" blue square.
- Stitch a blue and white B triangle to each side of the blue and white squares. Add a D to complete the corner block.

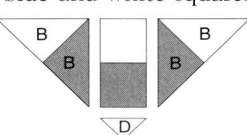

- Referring to the Assembly Diagram on page 9, lay out the blocks on point. Place the 12 setting and 4 corner blocks around the quilt. Place a 1" x 3" gray sashing strip between each block vertically and horizontally. Add a 1" white square at the sashing intersections.
- Stitch the blocks to the sashing in diagonal rows.
- Stitch diagonal rows of sashing and 1" squares.
- Join the block rows to the sashing rows.
- Trim the white squares diagonally at the quilt edges.
- Stitch the 1" x 17 1/2" gray strips to opposite sides of the quilt.
- Stitch the 1" x 18 1/2" gray strips to the remaining sides of the quilt.
- Finish referring to *Mini Stitching Tips* using 1 3/4" white strips for a continuous binding.

Shown on page 19

Gobble, Gobble,

Shopping for a good turkey?

QUILT SIZE 6" x 11 1/2"
BLOCK SIZE 3" x 3 1/2"

MATERIALS
Yardage is estimated for 44" fabric.
- Scraps of fall fabrics including a 3" square orange, for the beaks
- 1/4 yard of muslin or scraps of light fabrics, for the background
- 1 3/4" x 44" strip of autumn leaf fabric, for the binding
- 8" x 13 1/2" piece of backing fabric
- 8" x 13 1/2" piece of batting
- Clear template plastic
- 1 1/2" square of fusible webbing

PREPARATION
- Make full-size templates for the turkey parts. Place the plastic over the pattern pieces and trace the head, neck, wattle, belly, wings, feather and pumpkin and pumpkin stem. The beak is three dimensional and will be cut later.
- Trace around the templates on the right side of the appropriate fabric. Leave at least 3/8" between pieces. Add a 3/16" turn-under allowance all around each piece when cutting it out. Cut enough for 3 turkeys including 24 feathers in a variety of fabrics and 4 pumpkins with stems.
- Use a light box or brightly lit window and trace the Flying Geese patterns onto muslin or a light fabric. Make 2 of each strip.
- Select an orange scrap for the turkey beak and cut two 1 1/2" squares. Fuse the 1 1/2" orange squares wrong sides together using the fusible webbing.

CUTTING
In addition to the cutting done in Preparation, cut the following. Dimensions include 1/4" seam allowance.
- Cut 3: 1/4" squares, from the 1 1/2" fused orange, for the beaks
- Cut 3: 3 1/2" x 4" rectangles, assorted lights, for the turkey background
- Cut 4: 1 1/2" squares, light
- Cut 100: 1" squares, light
- Cut 50: 1" x 1 1/2", scraps of fall colors for the Flying Geese

DIRECTIONS
- Place the full-size turkey pattern between your light source and a 3 1/3" x 4" light rectangle. Trace around the turkey for fabric placement.
- Begin with the feathers and appliqué each in place using your needle to turn the 3/16" seam allowance under as you proceed. Complete the feathers.
- Next appliqué the wings and belly, then head, neck and wattle in this order, using the needle turn method.
- Fold each 1/4" orange beak square in half diagonally. Position the diagonal fold on the appliquéd seam between the head and throat just above the wattle.
- Stitch the beak along the diagonal fold line. Close the beak. Make 3 turkeys.
- Place a full-size pumpkin pattern between your light source and a 1 1/2" light square. Trace around the pumpkin for fabric placement.
- Appliqué the pumpkin stems in place, then the pumpkins. Make 4 pumpkins.
- Stitch the 3 turkeys together in a horizontal row.
- The Flying Geese border is stitched over a muslin foundation using the 1" squares of light and the 1" x 1 1/2" rectangles of fall colors. Position the fabric on the unmarked side of the muslin strip

Gobble

Full-Size Patterns for
Gobble, Gobble, Gobble

and stitch on the marked side. Begin at the bottom of a strip and pin a 1" x 1 1/2" rectangle over the first large triangle in position #1. Place a 1" light square in position #2 with the fabrics right side together. Pin in place. Turn the muslin foundation to the marked side and stitch on the line between position #1 and #2 avoiding the pins. Trim the seam to a scant 1/8". Finger press the triangle in place.

• Turn the foundation to the fabric side and place a 1" light square over the adjacent corner of the fall fabric rectangle, right sides together at position #3. Pin. Turn to the marked side and stitch in place along the line between position #1 and #3. Trim the seam. Finger press the triangle.

• Lay a 1" x 1 1/2" fall fabric rectangle right sides against the first Flying Geese block on the fabric sides of the foundation. Pin in place.

• Turn to the marked side and stitch on the line between position #4 and #2/#3. Trim the seam to 1/8". Finger press.

• Proceed adding light triangles to positions #5 and #6. Complete the 4 Flying Geese strips in this manner, trimming and pressing as you add each fabric.

• Lay out the 4 Flying Geese strips and the turkey row. Place a pumpkin in each corner. Stitch a pumpkin square to the ends of the short Flying Geese strips.

• Stitch a long Flying Geese strip to the top and bottom of the turkeys.

• Stitch a Flying Geese/pumpkin strip to the remaining sides of the turkeys.

• Finish as described in *Mini Stitching Tips* using the 1 3/4" x 44" autumn leaf strip for a continuous binding.

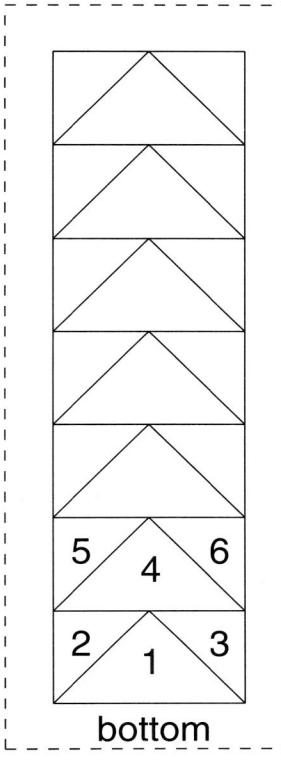

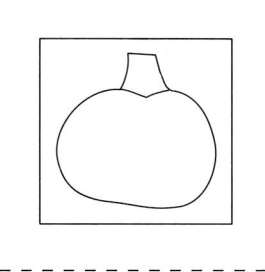

Pumpkin pattern

Flying Geese foundation patterns

Turkey pattern

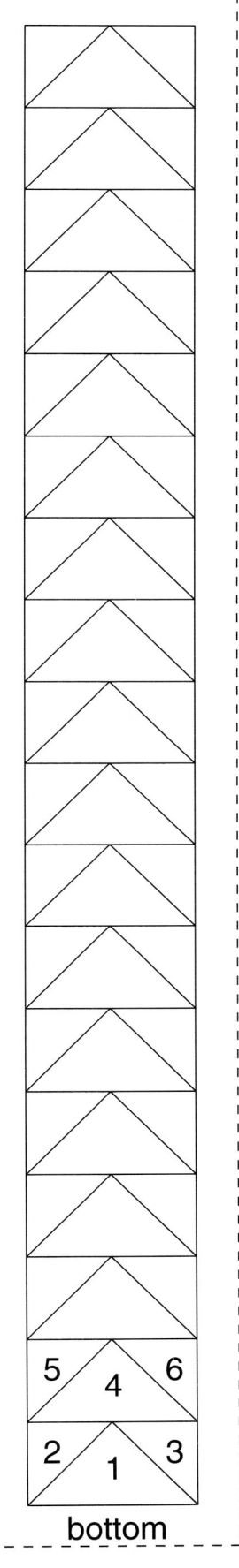

Shown on page 19

Boston "T" Party

A paper pieced beauty!

QUILT SIZE 14 1/4" x 16 1/2"
BLOCK SIZE 2 1/4"

MATERIALS
Yardage is estimated for 44" fabric.
- 1/2 yard of blue with stars
- 3/4 yard of cream
- 1/8 yard of red and cream striped
- 1/4 yard of muslin or non-woven interfacing for the foundations

CUTTING
Dimensions include 1/4" seam allowance.
- Cut 30: 3" squares, muslin or interfacing
- Cut 30: A, blue
- Cut 60: B, blue
- Cut 2: 1 3/4" x 18" strips, blue
- Cut 2: 1 3/4" x 15 3/4" strips, blue
- Cut 150: C, cream
- Cut 30: D, cream
- Cut 2: 1 3/4" x 44" strips, stripe

PREPARATION
- Lay a 3" muslin or interfacing square over the full-size pattern and trace all the lines and numbers onto the foundation. Make 30.

NOTE: *For foundation piecing, the fabrics are placed on the blank side of each foundation and stitched on the printed side.*

DIRECTIONS
- Center a blue A over position 1 on the unprinted side of the block foundation. Lay a cream C right sides together over A with the seam allowance extending between positions 1 and 2. Hold all the layers to the light to make sure that the raw edges of the fabric extend 1/4" beyond the seamline.
- Carefully turn the foundation to the printed side and stitch on the seamline between 1 and 2.
- Trim the seam to 1/8" and finger press the fabrics.
- Lay a cream C right side against A with the seam allowance extending between positions 1 and 3. Hold the fabric to the light and verify the 1/4" seam allowance.
- Flip the foundation over and stitch on the line between 1 and 3. Trim to 1/8" and finger press.
- Proceed in numerical order according to the numbers on the foundation. Use a blue B in positions 4 and 5, cream C's in positions 6, 7, and 8 and a cream D in position 9.
- Make all 30 blocks.
- Lay out the blocks in 5 rows of 6.
- Stitch the blocks into rows. Join the rows.
- Center and stitch the 1 3/4" x 15 3/4" blue strips to the short sides of the quilt. Start and stop stitching 1/4" from the ends.
- Center and stitch the 1 3/4" x 18" blue strips to each remaining quilt side. Start and stop stitching 1/4" from the ends.
- Miter each corner, referring to *Mini Stitching Tips* as needed.
- Finish according to *Mini Stitching Tips* using the 1 3/4" strips of striped fabric in a continuous binding.

Full-Size Patterns for Boston "T" Party

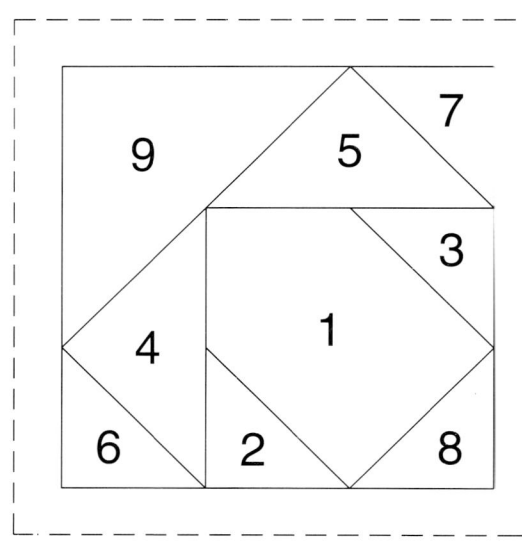
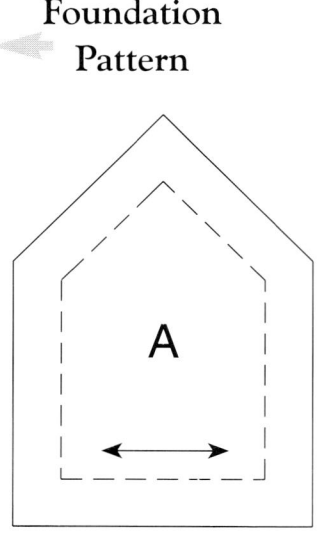

Foundation Pattern

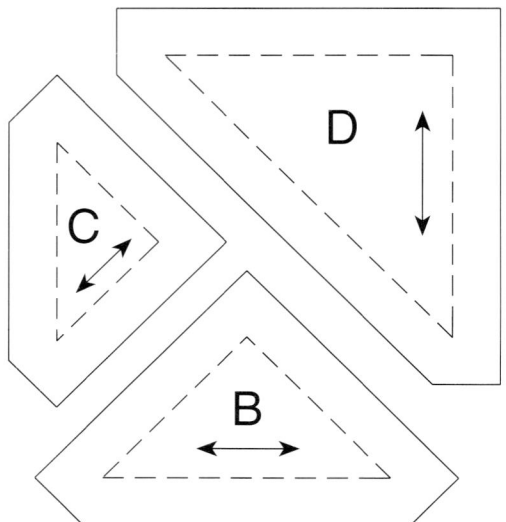

Cabins, Hearts and Scraps

A great way to play!

Shown on page 19

← *Full-Size Pattern*

QUILT SIZE 16 1/2" x 21 1/4"
BLOCK SIZE 4 1/4" square

MATERIALS
- 15" square of red homespun for the background and border
- Scraps of dark blue and maroon for the hearts and border
- Scrap lights for hearts
- 1 yard blue plaid for the sashing and binding
- 17 1/2" x 23" piece of backing fabric
- 17 1/2" x 23" piece of batting
- 12" square of muslin for the foundations
- 5" square of red

CUTTING
All dimensions include 1/4" seam allowance.
- Cut 6: 4" squares, muslin
- Cut 6: 4 3/4" squares, red homespun
- Cut 3: 1 5/8" x 4 3/4" strips, blue plaid
- Cut 2: 1 5/8" x 10 1/8" strips, blue plaid
- Cut 2: 1 5/8" x 15 1/2" strips, blue plaid
- Cut 2: 1 5/8" x 12 3/8" strips, blue plaid
- Cut 2: 1 3/4" x 44" strips, blue plaid, for the binding
- Cut 6: 1" squares, red, for the center
- Cut 6: 1" squares, light scrap, for position 2
- Cut 6: 1" x 1 1/2" rectangles, light, for position 3
- Cut 6: 1" x 2" rectangles, light, for position 6
- Cut 6: 1" x 2 1/2" rectangles, light, for position 7
- Cut 6: 1" x 3" rectangles, light, for position 10
- Cut 6: 1" x 3 1/2" rectangles, light, for position 11
- Cut 6: 1" x 1 1/2" rectangles, dark, for position 4
- Cut 6: 1" x 2" rectangles, dark, for position 5
- Cut 6: 1" x 2 1/2" rectangles, dark, for position 8
- Cut 6: 1" x 3" rectangles, dark, for position 9
- Cut 6: 1" x 3 1/2" rectangles, dark, for position 12
- Cut 6: 1" x 4" rectangles, dark, for position 13
- Cut 9: 2 7/8" squares, maroon, in half diagonally
- Cut 9: 2 7/8" squares, brown, in half diagonally

DIRECTIONS
NOTE: *Refer to the diagram and cutting instructions for fabric color and position.*
- Stitch a 1" red square to a 1" light square, right sides together along one side. Press.
- Stitch a 1" x 1 1/2" light rectangle to the red and light squares, in position 3, as shown.
- Stitch a 1" x 1 1/2" dark rectangle in position 4.
- Continue adding 1" light and dark rectangles around the block following the position numbers indicated on the diagram. Make 6 Log Cabin blocks.

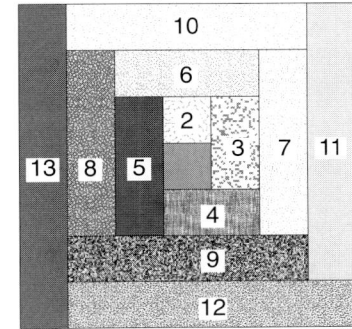

- Place the heart template over a completed Log Cabin block as shown in the diagram. The dark section of the Log Cabin block should be at the bottom of the heart.

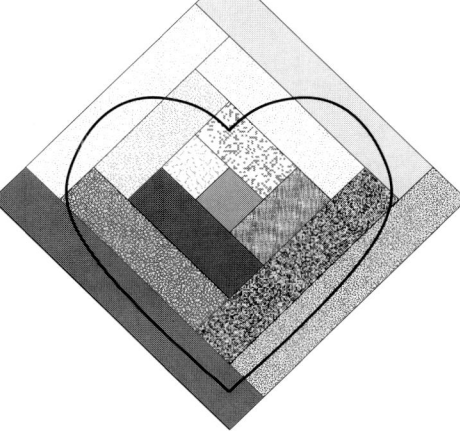

- Trace around the template.
- Cut the heart from the Log Cabin block adding a 3/16" turn-under allowance.

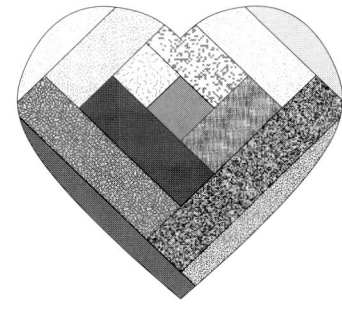

- Center and trace around the heart template on the right side of the six 4 3/4" red homespun squares.
- Appliqué the Log Cabin hearts to the red homespun squares using the tip of your needle to turn under the seam allowance and the drawn line as a placement guide.
- Stitch an appliquéd heart square to each long side of a 1 5/8" x 4 3/4" blue plaid strip making a heart row. Make 3 rows in this manner.

(continued)

Cabins, Hearts and Scraps
(continued)

- Stitch a 1 5/8" x 10 1/8" blue plaid strip horizontally between each of the 3 heart rows, as shown.

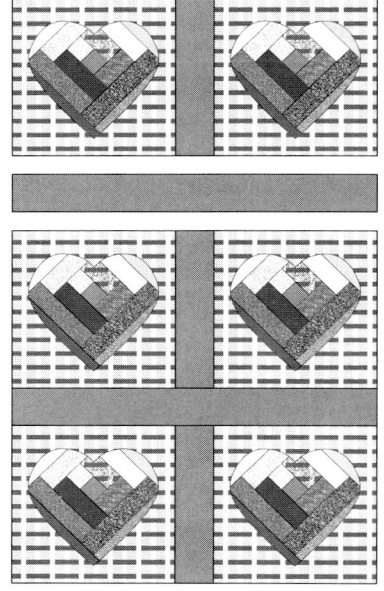

- Stitch the 1 5/8" x 15 1/2" blue plaid strips to the long sides of the quilt.
- Stitch the 1 5/8" x 12 3/8" blue plaid strips to the top and bottom.
- Stitch a maroon triangle to a brown triangle forming a pieced square. Make 18 pieced squares.
- Join 8 pieced squares to form a row, as shown. Make 2 pieced square rows.

- Make a pieced strip using 2 1/2" wide scrap pieces. Use the 2 left over maroon/brown pieced squares, if you desire. Stitch the scraps together to form a strip 2 1/2" x 17 3/4". Refer to the photo for ideas. Make 2.
- Stitch the pieced strips to the left and right sides of the quilt.
- Stitch the pieced square rows to the top and bottom of the quilt.
- Finish as described in *Mini Stitching Tips*, using the 1 3/4" blue plaid strips for the binding.

Soaring About

Spread your wings and fly with us!

QUILT SIZE 17 1/2" x 23 1/2"
BLOCK SIZE 3" square

MATERIALS
Yardage is estimated for 44" fabric.
- 1/4 yard of red
- 1/4 yard of light blue print
- 3/4 yard of solid blue
- 1 1/4 yards of white
- 20" x 26" piece of backing fabric
- 20" x 26" piece of batting

CUTTING
Dimensions include 1/4" seam allowance.
- Cut 48: A, red or cut twelve 2 1/4" squares in quarters diagonally
- Cut 100: B, solid blue or cut fifty 1 3/8" squares in half diagonally
- Cut 120: A, solid blue
- Cut 8: D, solid blue
- Cut 8: DR, solid blue
- Cut 3: 1 3/4" x 44" strips, solid blue for the binding
- Cut 12: 1 1/2" squares, light blue print
- Cut 72: A, light blue print or cut eighteen 2 1/4" squares in quarters diagonally
- Cut 16: B, light blue print or cut eight 1 3/8" squares in half diagonally
- Cut 32: DR, light blue print
- Cut 32: D, light blue print
- Cut 20: 1" squares, white
- Cut 32: 1 1/2" squares, white
- Cut 48: A, white or cut twelve 2 1/4" squares in quarters diagonally
- Cut 40: C, white
- Cut 500: B, white or cut two hundred fifty 1 3/8" squares in half diagonally
- Cut 2: 2 1/2" x 12 1/2" strips, white
- Cut 2: 2 1/2" x 6 1/2" strips, white
- Cut 2: 2" x 14 1/2" strips, white
- Cut 2: 2" x 23 1/2" strips, white

DIRECTIONS
- Stitch a white B to adjacent sides of a red A, as shown. Make 48 red Flying Geese.

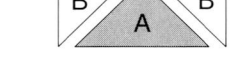

- Stitch a solid blue B to adjacent sides of a white A. Make 48 white Flying Geese.
- Stitch a white Flying Geese to a red Flying Geese exactly as shown. Make 48 pieced squares.

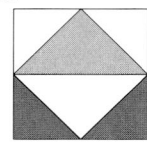

- Lay out Block 1 using 4 pieced squares, four 1 1/2" white squares and a 1 1/2" light blue print square, as shown. The 16 remaining pieced squares will be used in Block 2.

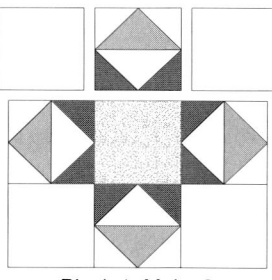

Block 1 Make 8

- Stitch the squares into rows. Join the rows. Make 8.
- Stitch Block 1 in pairs forming 4 rows.
- Join the rows.
- Stitch a white B to adjacent sides of a light blue print A. Make 72 light blue print Flying Geese.
- Stitch 6 light blue print Flying Geese together as shown. Repeat for a total of 4 six Geese units.

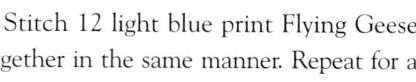

- Stitch 12 light blue print Flying Geese together in the same manner. Repeat for a total of 4 twelve Geese units.

America

Shown on page 19

- Join 2 six Geese units end to end so the points are facing the middle. Make 2 pieced rows exactly the same.
- Stitch a 2 1/2" x 6 1/2" white strip to the long side of each pieced row. Make 2 pieced rows.

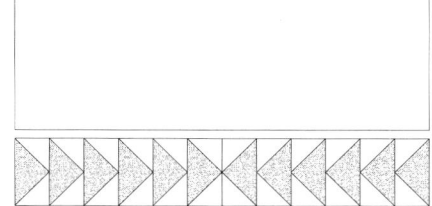

- Stitch a pieced unit to the short sides of the blocks.
- Join two 12-Geese units end to end so the points are facing the middle. Make 2.
- Stitch a 2 1/2" x 12 1/2" white strip to the long side of the pieced Geese rows. Make 2 pieced row units. Set aside.
- Stitch a light blue print D and DR to adjacent sides of a white C, as shown. Make 32.
- Stitch a light blue print B to a white B, as shown. Make 16.

- Lay out Block 2 using 8 C-D squares, 4 B-B squares, 4 pieced squares (originally made for Block 1), four 1" white squares and a 1 1/2" light blue print square.

Block 2 Make 4

- Stitch each of the four corner squares into a Four Patch before stitching the rows.
- Stitch the squares into 3 rows. Join the rows. Make 4 Block 2's.
- Stitch a Block 2 to each end of the Flying Geese pieced row units you have set aside.

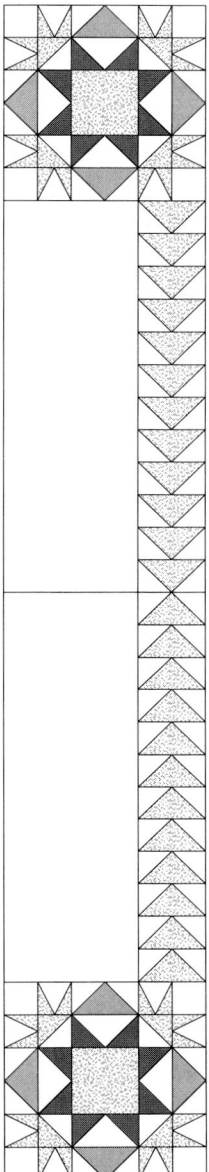

- Stitch a Block 2 row to each long side of the quilt keeping the Flying Geese against the quilt.
- Stitch a white B to adjacent sides of a blue A. Make 120 Flying Geese units.
- Stitch 4 rows of 12 Flying Geese. Point each unit in the same direction.
- Join 2 of the 12-unit Flying Geese rows together end to end so the Flying Geese point away from the center. Refer to the photo referencing the outer border. Make a second row in this manner.
- Stitch a Flying Geese row to each short side of the quilt.
- Stitch a blue B to a white B. Make 4.
- Stitch a blue D and DR to adjacent sides of a white C. Make 8.
- Make a Four Patch using a B-B square, 2 C-D squares and a 1" white square, as shown. Stitch the squares in pairs and join the pairs. Make 4.

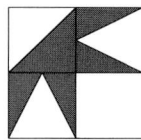

- Stitch 4 rows of 18 Flying Geese. Point each unit in the same direction.
- Join 2 of the 18 unit Flying Geese rows end to end so the Flying Geese point away from the center. Make 2 rows like this.
- Stitch a Four Patch to each end of the Flying Geese row. Place the Four Patches so that the white square will form the outside corner of the quilt.
- Stitch a Flying Geese row to each long side of the quilt.
- Stitch a 2" x 14 1/2" white strip to each short side of the quilt.
- Stitch a 2" x 23 1/2" white strip to each long side of the quilt.
- Finish as described in *Mini Stitching Tips* using the 1 3/4" blue strips to make a continuous binding.

Full-Size Patterns for Soaring About America

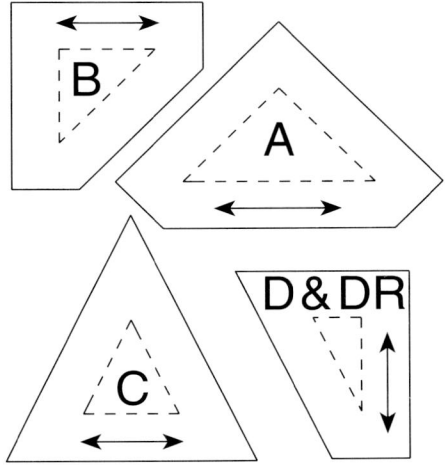

Old Tyme Puzzle

It's great fun to solve this winner!

Shown on page 20

QUILT SIZE 16" x 20"
BLOCK SIZE 3" square

MATERIALS
Yardage is estimated for 44" fabric.
- 32 dark/medium scraps at least 4" x 7"
- 1/2 yard of muslin for the background and border
- 1/4 yard of green for the outer border and binding
- 18" x 22" piece of backing fabric
- 18" x 22" piece of batting

CUTTING
Dimensions include 1/4" seam allowance. Group all like fabrics together as you cut.

From each of 18 fabrics:
- Cut 4: 1" squares
- Cut 1: 1 1/2" square
- Cut 4: A's or cut two 1 7/8" squares in half diagonally

From each of 14 fabrics:
- Cut 2: 1" squares
- Cut 1: A

Also:
- Cut 17: 1 1/2" squares, muslin
- Cut 96: 1" squares, muslin
- Cut 82: A, muslin or cut forty-one 1 7/8" squares in half diagonally
- Cut 2: 1 1/2" x 15 1/2" strips, muslin
- Cut 2: 1 1/2" x 13 1/2" strips, muslin
- Cut 2: 1 3/4" x 17 1/2" strips, green
- Cut 2: 1 3/4" x 16" strips, green
- Cut 2: 1 3/4" x 44" strips, green for the binding

DIRECTIONS
- Use a large cutting mat or similar flat surface or a design wall to arrange your fabrics. Following the Layout Diagram below, arrange the squares and half-squares from the 18 different fabrics in the Indiana Puzzle pattern using the muslin squares and half-squares to complete the design. Squares and half-squares from the additional 14 fabrics complete the border rows.
- Keep the pieces in the layout and remove four 1" squares at a time. Stitch the squares into pairs. Join the pairs. Replace the Four Patch in the layout. Repeat until all 1" squares are joined.
- Remove a scrap A and muslin A from the layout. Stitch the A's forming a pieced square. Return the pieced squares to the layout. Repeat this for all A's.
- Stitch the Four Patches, pieced squares and 1 1/2" squares into 11 rows of 15.
- Join the rows.
- Stitch the 1 1/2" x 15 1/2" muslin strips to the long sides of the quilt.
- Stitch the 1 1/2" x 13 1/2" muslin strips to the remaining sides of the quilt.
- Stitch the 1 3/4" x 17 1/2" green strips to the long sides.
- Stitch the 1 3/4" x 16" green strips to the remaining sides of the quilt.
- Finish as described in *Mini Stitching Tips* using the 1 3/4" green strips to make a continuous binding.

Layout Diagram

Full-Size Pattern

A

A Wrench in the Works

Shown on page 20

With just one "twist" of the wrench...

QUILT SIZE 11 1/2" x 13 1/2"
BLOCK SIZE 1 1/2"

MATERIALS
Yardage is estimated for 44" fabric.
- 1/3 yard red
- 1/2 yard white printed, bleached muslin
- 13 1/2" x 15 1/2" piece of fabric for backing
- 13 1/2" x 15 1/2" piece of batting

CUTTING
Dimensions include 1/4" seam allowance.
- Cut 4: C, red
- Cut 4: D, red
- Cut 2: 3/4" x 44" strips, red
- Cut 2: 1 3/8" x 35" strips, red
- Cut 2: 3/4" x 9" strips, red
- Cut 2: 3/4" x 11 1/2" strips, red
- Cut 2: 1 3/4" x 44" strips, red, for the binding
- Cut 1: A, white
- Cut 4: B, white
- Cut 2: 3/4" x 44" strips, white
- Cut 2: 1 3/8" x 35" strips, white
- Cut 24: 1" squares, white
- Cut 16: 1" x 2" rectangles, white
- Cut 3: 1" x 10" strips, white
- Cut 2: 1" x 8" strips, white
- Cut 2: 1" x 11" strips, white
- Cut 2: 1 1/2" x 9 1/2" strips, white
- Cut 2: 1 1/2" x 13 1/2" strips, white

DIRECTIONS
- Stitch a 3/4" x 44" red strip to a 3/4" x 44" white strip, right sides together down their length. Press the seam toward the red fabric. Make 2 pieced strips.
- Cut thirty-eight 1" slices from each pieced strip, for a total of 76.

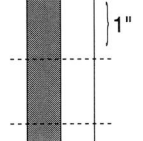

- Lay a 1 3/8" x 35" red strip on a 1 3/8" x 35" white strip, right sides together. Cut twenty 1 3/8" red and white squares from the strip. Repeat with another 1 3/8" x 35" red and 1 3/8" x 35" white strip. Cut a total of 38 units, treating a 1 3/8" red and a 1 3/8" white square as a single unit.
- Draw a diagonal line from corner to corner on the wrong side of each of the forty 1 3/8" white squares.
- Stitch a seam 1/4" to the left and right of the drawn diagonal line, as shown. You may use your presser foot as a guide or draw stitching lines.

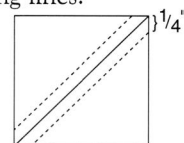

- Cut the squares apart along the center diagonal line. Trim the seams and press toward the red side. You will have 76 pieced squares.
- Lay out a block using 4 pieced squares, 4 red and white slices and a 1" white square, as shown.

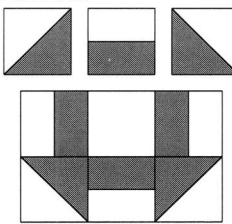

- Stitch the squares into 3 rows. Join the rows. Trim the seams to 1/8" as necessary. Make 19 blocks.
- To make the odd block, stitch a red C to a white B. Make 4.
- Stitch red D's to opposite sides of two B-C units. Make 2.

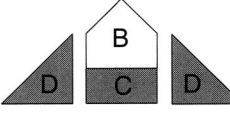

- Stitch a B-C unit to opposite sides of A. Join the three units as shown.

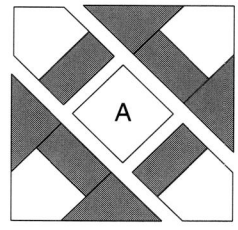

- Arrange the blocks in 5 rows of 4. Place a 1" x 2" white rectangle between the blocks in vertical rows. Join the blocks to the rectangles.
- Stitch a 1" x 10" white strip between each of the 4 completed vertical rows.
- Stitch a 1" x 8" white strip to the top and bottom, or short sides, of the quilt.
- Stitch a 1" x 11" white strip to the remaining sides of the quilt.
- Stitch a 3/4" x 9" red strip to the top and bottom, and then stitch a 3/4" x 11 1/2" red strip to the left and right sides of the quilt.
- Stitch a 1 1/2" x 9 1/2" white strip to the top and bottom, and a 1 1/2" x 13 1/2" white strip to the left and right sides of the quilt.
- Finish as described in *Mini Stitching Tips* and bind using 1 3/4" red strips.

Full-Size Patterns for A Wrench in the Works

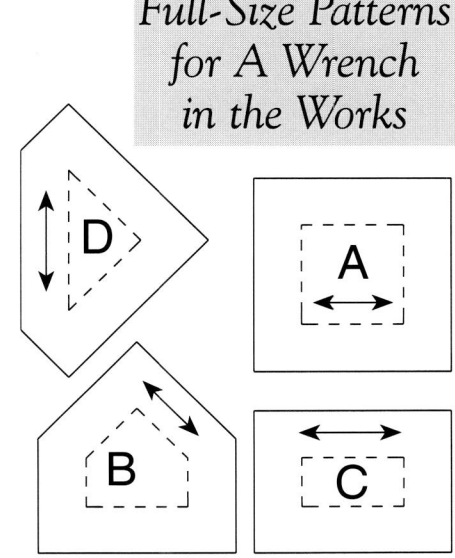

ON THE WALL:
"Log Cabin" (9" x 11"), by Kelly M. Forth, Peru, Indiana. Are you ready for a challenge? Kelly hand pieced this quilt using templates. We have presented the pattern in this way. The results will be thrilling and your handpiecing skills will grow with each block you complete. Choose fabrics that contrast with each other to give the quilt a traditional Log Cabin look. Pattern on page 6.

ON THE TABLE:
"My Amish Bars and Vines" (9" x 11 3/4"), by Bonnie Fought Offerle, Sheridan, Wyoming. Bonnie loves Amish colors and made this miniature "just for the fun of it." We were glad she did! The quilt combines strip piecing and appliqué. It will go together so quickly that you'll find yourself making more than one. Pattern on page 7.

ON THE WALL:
"March Madness" (23" square) by Sandra Gould, Sussex, New York, is "a tribute to the annual NCAA basketball tournament. There are 64 baskets, each a different fabric, which represent the 64 teams participating in the first round of the tournament." Pattern on page 8.

ON THE TABLE:
"Honey, I Shrunk the Quilt" (18 1/2" square) by Ruth Hughes Adams, Essex, Connecticut. Ruth writes, "The original of this quilt (72" square) almost slipped away from the family at a tag sale. We feel blessed to own it. My husband's great, great grandmother made it. She was born in 1808, the same year Mary Todd Lincoln was born." Pattern on page 9.

"Gobble, Gobble, Gobble" (6" x 11 1/2") by Sharron Lambert, Bedford, Michigan. These little guys will steal your heart. If all turkeys look like the three Sharron designed, it would be fruit and vegetables for Thanksgiving from now on. Sharron could not find many Thanksgiving decorations so she made her own, basing this quilt on a large carved turkey she purchased from a country store. Pattern on page 10.

UPPER LEFT:
"Boston "T" Party" (14 3/4" x 17") by Madeline Scoda, Tampa, Florida. Madeline recently discovered paper foundation piecing. This square suited her to a "T". Foundation work lends itself to take-along projects. This is a good place to start. Pattern on page 12.

UPPER RIGHT:
"Cabins, Hearts and Scraps" (15 1/2" x 21"), by Cheri Henning, Colden, New York. Cheri has successfully combined piecing and appliqué with a traditional old-time look. There is plenty of room for you to be creative and make this quilt uniquely yours. See page 13 for the pattern.

LOWER LEFT:
"Soaring About America" (17" x 22") by Dorothy Schwolow, Berwyn, Illinois. The red, white and blue stars made Dorothy feel patriotic. She "imagined the geese soaring about America." Wrote Dorothy, "This all started when I was reading Miniature Quilts, Winter 1991. I needed to Fly the Coop." Escape with us, pattern on page 14.

LOWER RIGHT:
"A Wrench in the Works" see picture on page 20.

UPPER LEFT: "Olde Tyme Puzzle" (16" x 20") by Carol Sherrill, East Granby, Connecticut. Although the Indiana Puzzle Block is not difficult to construct, Carol's version of this old favorite is a challenge to execute. A fabric saver's delight, the quilt must be completely laid out before construction can begin. Carol especially chose her fabrics to look "olde". Pattern on page 16.

LOWER LEFT: "A Wrench in the Works" (11 1/2" x 13 1/2") by Shanna Smith Suttner, Chesterfield, Missouri. Shanna has a wonderful sense of humor. Look closely at her quilt. She used the Monkey Wrench block but there is a "wrench" in there. We give you the pattern (on page 17) for this red and white beauty, monkeywrench and all.

LOWER MIDDLE:
"Spools Everywhere" (18 3/4" square) by Sarah Francis of Douglas, Texas. This quilt looks like a piecing nightmare, but not to worry! We have step-by-step directions that will have you threading through the block with confidence. Sarah miniaturized this block from a large quilt pattern handed down from friend to friend. She discovered, however, the pattern also appeared in Miniature Quilts Issue #4. This is a quilt that requires fun fabrics. Sarah shares her quilting design, too. What is it? What else, a spool! Pattern on page 25.

CENTER TOP: "Star Tricks" (14 3/4" x 18 3/4") by Doris Wells, Wilmington, Delaware. This fun version of the Card Tricks block assembles in a Nine Patch fashion. The wonderful border looks more complicated than it is, but it, too, is based on that familiar Nine Patch. Stand back and smile as your friends wonder "How did she do that?" We will show you on page 26.

FAR RIGHT: "Hunter's Star" (14 3/4" x 18 1/2") by Pat Chase of Sumner, Washington. This quilt is especially designed for the handwork enthusiast. Pat writes, "The piecing is all by hand as I could find no quicker way to complete it." This beautiful mini is presented in only two colors. The art is in the construction. It's a great carry-along project. Need a challenge? See page 24.

LOWER RIGHT: "Stacked Bricks" (16" x 16 1/2") by Monica C. Tomka of Howells, Nebraska. Monica used purple hues in this true miniature version of a large quilt. The border fabric adds to the visual excitement. We show you a piecing technique that makes a perfect quilt every time. You will want to make a stack of these miniatures! See page 37 for the pattern.

ON THE TABLE: "Quilter's Dream" (21" x 24") by June Kempston, Orchard Park, New York. The first contest June has entered was quite a challenge. She miniaturized the 12" Quilter's Dream block that is pictured in Judy Martin's Scraps, Blocks and Quilts, Patterns & Techniques, (Crosley-Griffith Publishing Co., Inc., 1990). Pattern on page 28.

ON THE WALL:
"Autumn Engagement" (18 1/2" x 26 1/2") by Sarah Francis of Douglass, Texas, was made "to celebrate the 13th anniversary of the day my husband proposed to me.... We were in a state park in Oklahoma and the leaves were ablaze with color." Sarah scaled down a design from More Template-Free Quiltmaking by Trudie Hughes (That Patchwork Place, 1987). Our pattern for this small version is on page 30.

ON THE TABLE:
"Antiquated Nine Patch" (19 1/2" x 23 1/2") by Karen L. Bockelman, Portland, Oregon. The paisley border fabric inspired this antique-looking Nine Patch. Fabric selection and quilting give this miniature that turn-of-the-century look. Just what Karen had in mind! The pattern is given on page 29.

"Silk Memories" (9" x 10 1/2") by Anna B. Scott, Fairfax Station, Virginia. Anna's original design uses her "grandmother's antique silk thread and scraps from a tie factory. The dates, names, and places embroidered on the quilt represent special family memories." This quilt is sheer joy to make. You are free to embroider and embellish to your heart's content. Record your own memories. Pattern on page 32.

RIGHT: "Windblown Lily" (13 1/2" x 17 3/4") by Amanda G. Beahm, Timberville, Virginia. "The idea for reducing this block (to 3") came while I spent time on our riding lawnmower," wrote Amanda. She then developed this into a workshop to show how an idea can grow. What's next? "I have reduced this block even smaller—to 1 1/2"." This delicate quilt would be a unique addition to any home. Pattern begins on page 34.

UPPER LEFT:
"Magnolia" (18" x 22") by Jean Keener, Ashland, Ohio. This is an adaptation of the Poinsettia Basket, by Sylvia Trygg Voudrie, Tiny Traditions (Chitra Publications, 1992). Jean is responsible for the miniatures display in her guild's annual show. Although she waited until the show's conclusion in June to begin this miniature, the result was excellent. This quilt needed to be shared. What color choices will you make for your Magnolia buds? Pattern on page 36.

ON THE TABLE:
"Raspberry Confetti" (21 1/4" square) by Jeanne Marynowski, Scottsdale, Arizona. In her first miniature Jeanne successfully combined two traditional patterns. The Bear's Paw and Variable Star join together and develop movement and interest. The star is formed in the sashing that surrounds the Bear's Paw. This quilt holds your attention from start to finish. Pattern on page 38.

Hunter's Star

Pieced by hand or machine—a rewarding effort.

Shown on page 21

QUILT SIZE 14 3/4" x 18 1/2"
BLOCK SIZE 1 7/8"

MATERIALS

Yardage is estimated for 44" fabric.
- 1/2 yard of blue floral
- 1/2 yard of white
- 1/4 yard of light blue for first border and binding
- 17" x 20" piece of backing fabric
- 17" x 20" piece of batting
- 5" square of clear template plastic

CUTTING

Pattern pieces include 1/4" seam allowance as do all dimensions given. Trim seams to 1/8" after sewing.
- Cut 2: 1 1/2" x 15 1/2" strips, blue floral
- Cut 2: 1 1/2" x 20" strips, blue floral
- Cut 48: A, blue floral or cut twenty-four 2 1/8" squares in half diagonally
- Cut 48: B, blue floral
- Cut 96: C, blue floral
- Cut 48: A, white, or cut twenty-four 2 1/8" squares in half diagonally
- Cut 48: B, white
- Cut 96: C, white
- Cut 2: 1" x 15 1/2" strips, light blue
- Cut 2: 1" x 20" strips, light blue
- Cut 2: 1 3/4" x 44" strips, light blue, for the binding

DIRECTIONS

- Lay out the pieces for a block using a blue A, a white A, a blue B, a white B, 2 blue C's and 2 white C's.

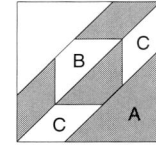

- Stitch a blue B between white C's, as shown. Finger press the seams toward the blue.
- Stitch a blue A to the B-C unit, as shown. Make 48 blue pieced triangles.
- Stitch a white B between blue C's. Finger press the seams toward the blue.
- Stitch a white A to the B-C unit. Make 48 white pieced triangles.
- Join a white pieced triangle to a blue pieced triangle matching the points carefully. Complete 48 blocks.
- Lay out 4 blocks, as shown. Rotate the blocks until the star pattern is visible in the center.

- Stitch the blocks into pairs. Join the pairs. Make 12 units using 4 blocks in each.
- Lay out the 12 units in 4 rows of 3.
- Stitch the units into rows. Join the rows.
- Stitch a 1" x 15 1/2" light blue strip to a 1 1/2" x 15 1/2" blue floral strip. Make 2 pieced strips.
- Center and stitch the pieced strips to the short sides of the quilt with the light blue strip against the quilt. Start and stop stitching 1/4" from the edge of the quilt.
- Stitch a 1" x 20" light blue strip to a 1" x 20" blue floral strip. Make 2 pieced strips.
- Center and stitch the pieced strips to the remaining sides of the quilt keeping the light blue strip against the quilt. Start and stop stitching 1/4" from the edge.
- Miter each corner following the directions in *Mini Stitching Tips* as needed.
- Finish using instructions in *Mini Stitching Tips*. Use the 1 3/4" light blue strips to make a continuous binding.

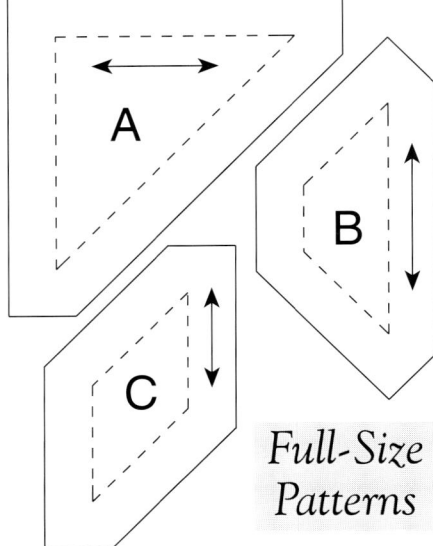

Full-Size Patterns

Rotary Cut Pattern Pieces

- You may prefer to cut B by first cutting a 1 3/4" x 44" strip of fabric. Cut twenty-four 1 3/4" squares from the strip. Cut each square in half diagonally. Lay the B template over the triangle and cut away the fabric not covered by the template.
- To rotary cut C, cut five 1" strips of fabric. Place your ruler's 45° line along the fabric edge with the left edge of the ruler at the far left corner of the strip. Trim the fabric to the left of the ruler as shown.

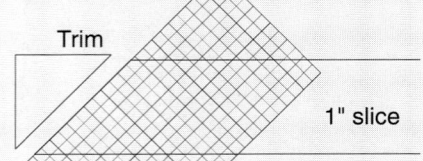

- Use the diagonal cut as your measuring point and cut 1" diagonal slices. Cut 96 from the 5 strips.

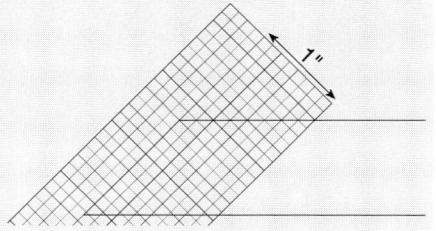

Spools Everywhere

Shown on page 20

Fun fabrics add to the joy of creating this mini!

QUILT SIZE 18 1/2" square
BLOCK SIZE 4" square

MATERIALS
Yardage is estimated for 44" fabric.
- 1/8 yard of pink
- 1/8 yard of blue
- 1/8 yard of burgundy
- 1/8 yard of turquoise
- 1/2 yard of light blue
- 1/2 yard of light print
- 1/8 yard of rose, for the first border and binding
- 1/4 yard of blue spool print
- 1 1/2" square of template plastic

PREPARATION
- Cover the full-size pattern with the clear template plastic. Transfer all lines to the template with permanent marker.

CUTTING
- Cut 2: 1 3/8" x 22" strips, pink
- Cut 1: 1 3/8" x 44" strip, pink
- Cut 2: 1 3/8" x 22" strips, blue
- Cut 1: 1 3/8" x 44" strip, blue
- Cut 2: 1 3/8" x 22" strips, burgundy
- Cut 1: 1 3/8" x 44" strip, burgundy
- Cut 2: 1 3/8" x 22" strips, turquoise
- Cut 1: 1 3/8" x 44" strip, turquoise
- Cut 8: 1 3/8" x 44" strips, light blue
- Cut 4: 7/8" x 22" strips, light print
- Cut 6: 7/8" x 44" strips, light print
- Cut 2: 1" x 12 1/2" strips, rose
- Cut 2: 1" x 13 1/2" strips, rose
- Cut 2: 3" x 13 1/2" strips, blue print
- Cut 2: 3" x 18 1/2" strips, blue print
- Cut 2: 1 3/4" x 44" strips, blue print, for the binding

DIRECTIONS
- Stitch a 7/8" x 44" light print strip between 1 3/8" x 44" light blue strips, as shown. Make 2 pieced strips in this manner.

- Position the clear template over the pieced strip aligning the light print strip between the lines on the template. Trace around the template. Reverse it, trace again. Trace around the template 18 times on each pieced strip. Cut the squares out. Label them A.

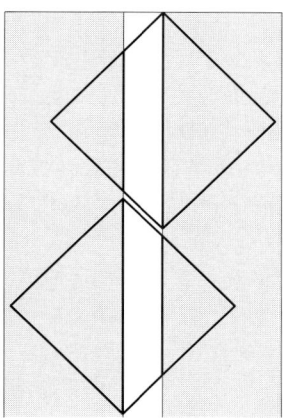

- Stitch a 7/8" x 44" light print strip between a 1 3/8" x 44" pink strip and a 1 3/8" x 44" light blue strip.
- Position the template over the pieced strip, aligning the light print strip between the lines on the template. Trace around the template. Reverse it, trace again for a total of 18. Cut them out. Label the 9 squares with a large pink triangle, B. Label the 9 squares with a large blue triangle, C.
- Stitch a 7/8" x 44" light print strip between a 1 3/8" x 44" blue strip and a 1 3/8" x 44" light blue strip.
- Position the template. Trace. Reverse. Cut out. Label the 9 squares with the large blue triangle, D. Label the 9 squares with the large light blue triangle, E.
- Stitch a 7/8" x 44" light print strip between a 1 3/8" x 44" burgundy strip and a 1 3/8" x 44" light blue strip.
- Position the template. Trace. Reverse. Trace and cut out. Label the 9 squares with the large light blue triangles, F. Label the 9 squares with the large burgundy triangle, G.
- Stitch a 7/8" x 44" light print strip between a 1 3/8" x 44" turquoise strip and a 1 3/8" x 44" light blue strip.
- Position the template. Trace. Reverse. Trace and cut out. Label the 9 squares with the large light blue triangle, H. Label the 9 squares with the large turquoise triangle, J.

Stitch 22" strips into the following pieced strips:
- Pink/light print/turquoise* Label K.
- Blue/light print/pink* Label L.
- Turquoise/light print/burgundy* Label M.
- Burgundy/light print/blue* Label N.
- Position the template with the small triangle edge extending over the fabric with the *. **Do Not** reverse the template. Trace around the template 9 times. Cut the squares out. Label them as indicated.
- Lay out a block in 4 rows of 4 squares following the block placement diagram.

(continued)

Block Placement Diagram

Spools Everywhere
(continued)

- Stitch the squares into rows. Join the rows. Make 9 blocks.
- Lay out the 9 blocks in 3 rows of 3. You can place each block the same or turn it 1/4 or 1/2 turn. Play with the block until you are pleased.
- Stitch the blocks into rows. Join the rows.
- Stitch the 1" x 12 1/2" rose strips to opposite sides of the quilt.
- Stitch the 1" x 13 1/2" rose strips to the remaining sides of the quilt.
- Stitch the 3" x 13 1/2" blue print strips to opposite sides of the quilt.
- Stitch the 3" x 18 1/2" blue print strips to the remaining sides of the quilt.
- Finish as described in *Mini Stitching Tips* using 1 3/4" blue print strips for binding.

Full-Size Pattern for Spools Everywhere

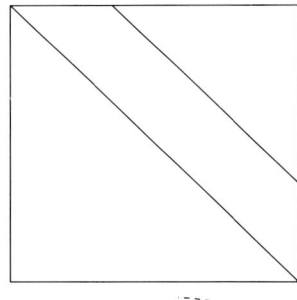

Quilting Design

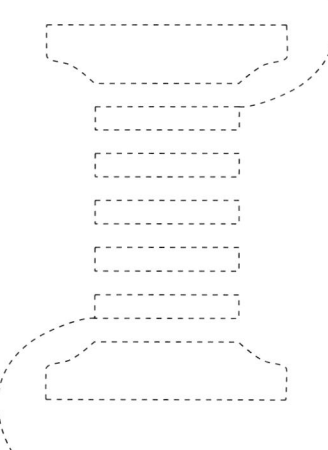

Star Tricks

Shown on page 21

Use Nine Patch construction and reach for the stars!

QUILT SIZE 14 3/4" x 18 3/4"
BLOCK SIZE 3" square

MATERIALS
Yardage is estimated for 44" fabric.
- 5" x 18" strip of red
- Quilter's quarter (18" x 22") of purple
- 4" x 16" strip of blue
- 11" x 18" rectangle of green
- 1/2 yard of cream
- 10" x 22" piece of green and red print, for the border
- 17" x 21" piece of backing fabric
- 17" x 21" piece of batting
- 2" square of template plastic

PREPARATION
- Trace pattern piece A onto clear template plastic with a permanent marker.

CUTTING
All dimensions include 1/4" seam allowance.
- Cut 5: 1" x 15" strips, cream
- Cut 96: 1 1/2" squares, cream
- Cut 3: 5 1/2" squares, cream, cut in quarters diagonally for the setting triangles. You will need 10 of the 12 triangles cut.
- Cut 4: 1" x 18" strips, cream
- Cut 1: 1" x 15" strip, green
- Cut 32: 1" squares, green
- Cut 4: 1 1/2" squares, green
- Cut 1: 1" x 10" strip, green
- Cut 1: 1" x 15" strip, red
- Cut 1: 1" x 10" strip, red
- Cut 2: 1 1/4" x 18" strips, red
- Cut 2: 1" x 15" strips, blue
- Cut 1: 1" x 10" strip, blue
- Cut 1: 1" x 15" strip, purple
- Cut 1: 1" x 10" strip, purple
- Cut 4: 1 3/4" x 22" strips, purple, for the binding
- Cut 2: 2" x 17" strips, green and red print, for the border
- Cut 2: 2" x 21" strips, green and red print, for the border

DIRECTIONS
- Stitch a 1" x 15" cream strip to a 1" x

Assembly Diagram

- 15" green strip right sides together down their long side. Press the seam away from the cream.
- Cut eight 1 1/2" slices from the pieced strip.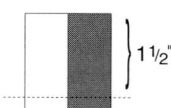
- Stitch a 1" x 15" cream strip to a 1" x 15" red strip right sides together, down their length. Repeat using a 1" x 15" cream strip stitched to a 1" x 15" blue strip, and a 1" x 15" cream strip stitched to a 1" x 15" purple strip. Cut eight 1 1/2" slices from each of the 3 pieced strips.
- Stitch a 1" x 10" red strip to a 1" x 10" purple strip down their long side. Press the seams toward the red.
- Cut eight 1" slices from the pieced strip.
- Stitch a 1" x 10" green strip to a 1" x 10" blue strip down their long side. Press the seam toward the blue.
- Cut eight 1" slices from the pieced strip.
- Stitch a 1" purple and red slice to a 1" blue and green slice to form a Four Patch, as shown. Make 8.
- Lay out a block using a Four Patch; a 1 1/2" pieced square of cream with green, cream and blue, cream and red, cream and purple; and four 1 1/2" cream squares, as shown.

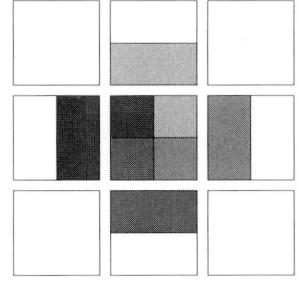

- Stitch the squares into rows. Join the rows. Make 8 for the inner quilt blocks.
- Stitch a 1" x 15" cream strip to a 1" x 15" blue strip right sides together along their length. Press away from the cream.
- Cut twelve 1" slices from the pieced strip.
- Stitch the pieced slices into pairs to form a Four Patch, alternating the cream and blue squares.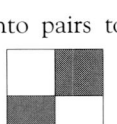

- Stitch a 1 1/4" x 18" red strip between 1" x 18" cream strips. Make 2.
- Lay template A over the pieced strip, lining up the seamlines on the fabric with the drawn lines on the template. Trace around the template 7 times on each pieced strip. Cut out the 14 A squares.

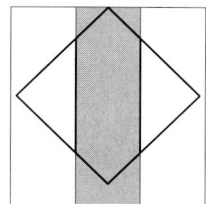

- Make 6 border blocks as follows. For each block, lay out six 1 1/2" cream squares, 2 blue and cream Four Patches and an A square, in 3 rows of 3 exactly as shown. Stitch the squares into rows. Join the rows. Make 6.

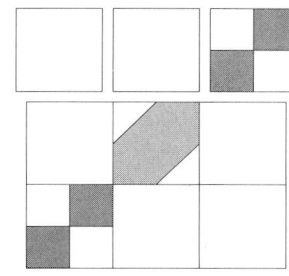

- Lay a 1" green square in adjacent corners of a 1 1/2" cream square. Stitch along the diagonal of the green squares. Trim to 1/4" seam allowance. Make 16 Star-point squares.

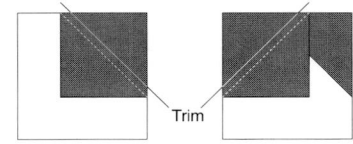

Full-Size Pattern for Star Tricks

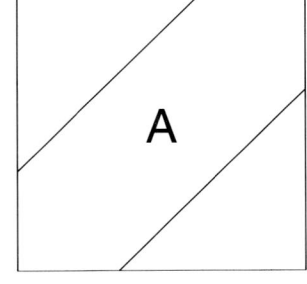

Quilting Design →

- Make 4 corner Nine Patches using 4 Star-point squares, two 1 1/2" cream squares, 2 A squares and a 1 1/2" green square. Arrange the squares exactly as shown. Stitch the squares into rows. Join the rows.

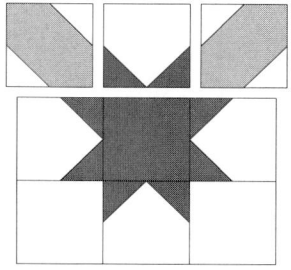

- Refer to the Assembly Diagram and lay out the 8 inner quilt blocks on point with the 6 border blocks around the sides and the 4 corner blocks in place. Arrange the setting triangles between the border blocks and a 1 1/2" cream square at each corner.
- Stitch the blocks in diagonal rows. Join the rows. To even the edges of the quilt trim 1/4" from the corner squares, as shown in the Assembly Diagram.
- Center and stitch the 2" x 17" green and red print strips to the short sides of the quilt. Start and stop stitching 1/4" from the quilt edge.
- Center and stitch the 2" x 21" green and red print strips to the remaining sides. Start and stop stitching 1/4" from the edge.
- Miter the corners, referring to the instructions in *Mini Stitching Tips*.
- Finish as described in *Mini Stitching Tips*. Use the 1 3/4" x 44" purple strips to make a continuous binding.

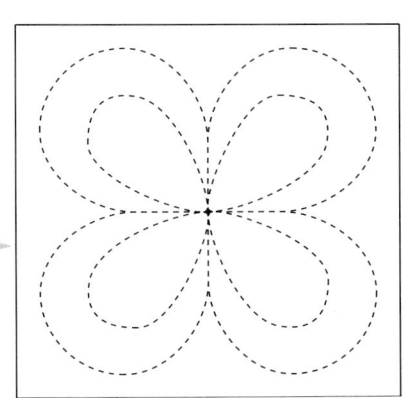

Quilter's Dream
A scrap collector's delight!

QUILT SIZE 21" x 24"
BLOCK SIZE 3" square

MATERIALS
Yardage is estimated for 44" fabric.
- 7" square of fabric for each of 20 stars
- 1/3 yard of cream for the star background
- 1/3 yard of tan print for the squares around the stars and middle border
- 1/8 yard of beige
- 1/2 yard of burgundy for inner and outer border and binding
- 23" x 25" piece of batting
- 23" x 25" piece of backing fabric

CUTTING
Dimensions include 1/4" seam allowance.
- Cut 4: 1" x 44" strips, tan print
- Cut 3: 1 1/2" x 22" strips, tan print
- Cut 2: 1" x 17" strips, tan print
- Cut 2: 1" x 19 1/2" strips, tan print
- Cut 2: 1" x 44" strips, beige
- Cut 6: 1 1/2" x 22" strips, beige
- Cut 2: 1" x 44" strips, cream
- Cut 80: A, cream
- Cut 2: 1" x 16" strips, burgundy
- Cut 2: 1" x 18 1/2" strips, burgundy
- Cut 2: 2 1/2" x 20 1/2" strips, burgundy
- Cut 2: 2 1/2" x 21" strips, burgundy
- Cut 3: 1 3/4" x 44" strips, burgundy, for the binding

For each of 20 stars:
- Cut 8: B
- Cut 1: 1 1/2" square
- Cut 2: 1" squares

DIRECTIONS
- Stitch a 1" x 44" tan print strip to a 1" x 44" beige strip, right sides together down their length. Press the seam toward the tan print. Make 2 pieced strips.
- Lay the pieced strip on a cutting mat and cut forty 1" slices from each pieced strip, for a total of 80.

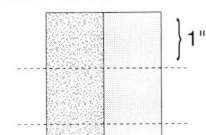

- Stitch a 1" x 44" tan print strip to a 1" x 44" cream strip, right sides together down their length. Press the seam toward the tan print. Make 2.
- Cut forty 1" slices from each pieced strip, for a total of 80.
- Stitch a tan and beige pair to a tan and cream pair forming a Four Patch, as shown. Alternate the tan squares. Make 80 Four Patches.

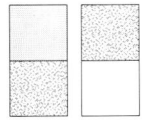

- For each of 20 Star Blocks lay out 4 Four Patches, 4 cream A's, 8 B's, and a 1 1/2" square for the star center, as shown.

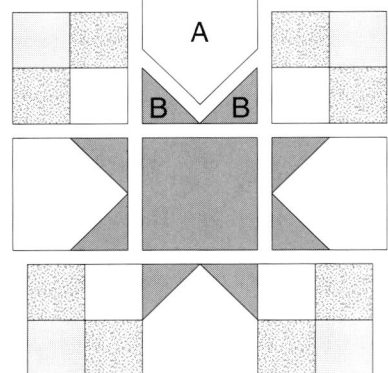

- Stitch a B to the adjacent sides of A at the point. Repeat for all 4 A's. Replace the pieced A's in the layout.
- Stitch a pieced A between 2 Four Patches. Make 2 rows in this manner.
- Stitch a 1 1/2" square between 2 pieced A's for the middle row. Join the rows to complete a Star Block. Make 20 Star Blocks.
- Stitch a 1 1/2" x 22" tan print strip between 1 1/2" x 22" beige strips. Press the seams toward the tan print. Make 3 pieced strips.
- Cut a total of forty-nine 1" slices from the 3 pieced strips, for sashing strips.
- Lay out the 20 Star blocks in 5 rows of 4, adding sashing strips between the blocks and at the end of each row.
- Stitch the blocks and strips completing 5 rows.
- Stitch a sashing row alternating 4 sashing strips and five 1" colored squares. Use the colored squares at random. Make 6 sashing rows in this manner. You will have 10 extra colored squares to use in another project.
- Stitch the sashing rows between the star rows and to the top and bottom of the quilt.
- Stitch the 1" x 18 1/2" burgundy strips to the long sides of the quilt.
- Stitch the 1" x 16" burgundy strips to the top and bottom of the quilt.
- Stitch the 1" x 19 1/2" tan print strips to the long sides of the quilt.
- Stitch the 1" x 17" tan print strips to the top and bottom of the quilt.
- Stitch the 2 1/2" x 20 1/2" burgundy strips to the sides and the 2 1/2" x 21" burgundy strips to the top and bottom of the quilt.
- Finish as described in *Mini Stitching Tips* using the 1 3/4" burgundy strips to make a continuous binding.

Full-Size Patterns

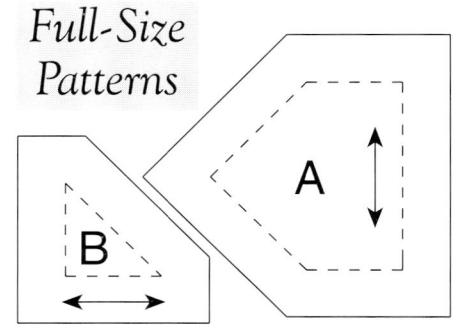

Antiquated Nine-Patch

Shown on page 22

Use new fabrics and create an old look!

QUILT SIZE 19 1/2" x 23 1/4"
BLOCK SIZE 2 5/8"

MATERIALS

Yardage is estimated for 44" fabric.
- 5" squares of 20 antique looking lights
- 5" squares of 20 antique looking darks
- 1/8 yard burgundy for the plain squares
- 1/8 yard brown plaid for the setting and corner triangles
- 1/4 yard dark print for the inner border and binding
- 1/8 yard paisley for the outer border
- 21 1/2" x 25 1/4" piece of backing fabric
- 21 1/2" x 25 1/4" piece of batting

CUTTING

Dimensions include 1/4" seam allowance.
For each of 20 Nine Patches:
- Cut 5: 1 3/8" squares, light
- Cut 4: 1 3/8" squares, dark

Also:
- Cut 12: 3 1/8" squares, burgundy
- Cut 4: 5" squares, brown plaid in quarters diagonally, you will need 14 of the 16 triangles. If you prefer cut 14 A's.
- Cut 2: 2 3/4" squares, brown plaid in half diagonally, or cut 4 B's.
- Cut 2: 3/4" x 15 1/2" strips, dark print
- Cut 2: 3/4" x 19 3/4" strips, dark print
- Cut 2: 2 1/4" x 16" strips, paisley
- Cut 2: 2 1/4" x 23 1/4" strips, paisley
- Cut 2: 1 3/4" x 44" strips, dark print for the binding

DIRECTIONS

For each of the 20 Nine Patch blocks:
- Lay out each Nine Patch block using five 1 3/8" light squares and four 1 3/8" dark squares, as shown in 3 rows of 3.

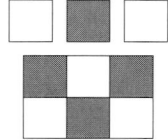

- Stitch the squares in rows. Join the rows.
- Make 20 Nine Patch blocks.
- Lay out the 20 Nine Patch blocks on point. Place the twelve 3 1/8" burgundy squares between the Nine Patches. Place setting triangles and corner triangles around the quilt.

- Stitch the triangles and squares into diagonal rows. Join the rows.
- Stitch a 3/4" x 15 1/2" dark print strip to the short sides of the quilt.
- Stitch a 3/4" x 19 3/4" dark print strip to the remaining sides of the quilt.
- Stitch a 2 1/4" x 16" paisley strip to the short sides and a 2 1/4" x 23 1/4" paisley strip to the remaining sides of the quilt.
- Finish as described in *Mini Stitching Tips* using the 1 3/4" dark print strips for the binding.

Full-Size Patterns for Antiquated Nine-Patch

Quilting Design

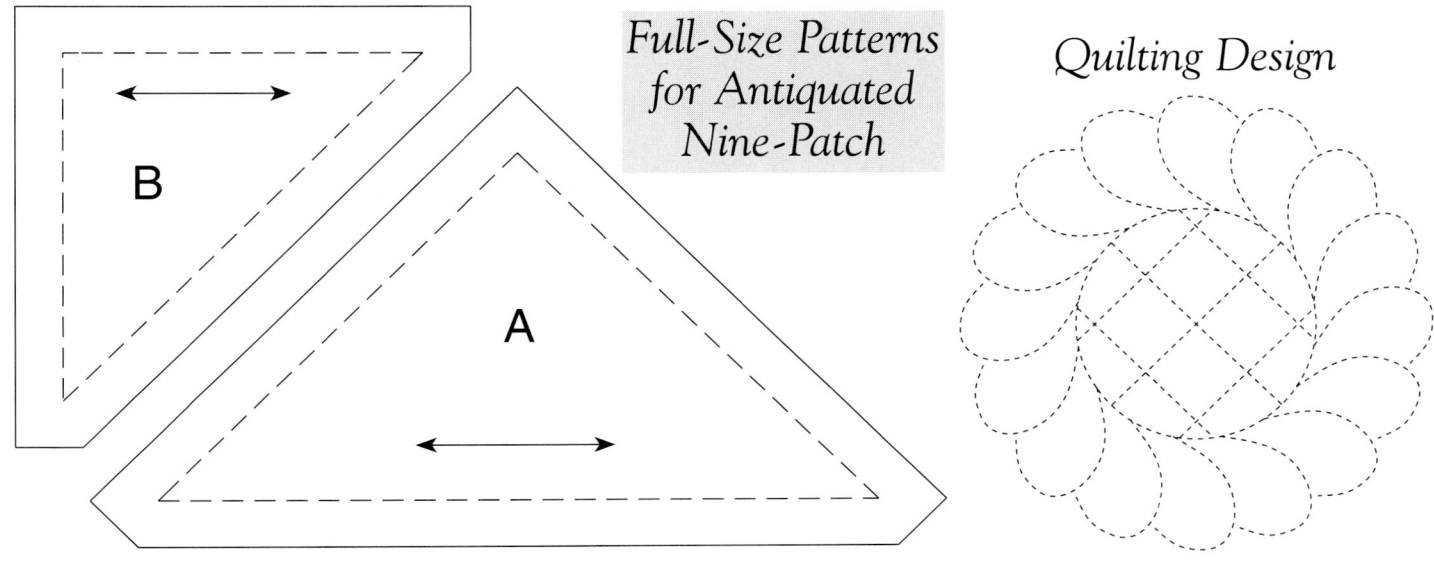

Shown on page 22

♥ Autumn Engagement

Easy piecing for an engaging quilt!

QUILT SIZE 18 3/4" x 26 3/4"
BLOCK SIZE 3" square

MATERIALS
Yardage is estimated for 44" fabric.
- 1/4 yard of gold
- 1/3 yard of light print
- 1/4 yard of burgundy
- 1/2 yard of leaf print
- 3/4 yard of dark fabric
- 21" x 29" piece of backing fabric
- 21" x 29" piece of batting

CUTTING
Dimensions include 1/4" seam allowance.
- Cut 35: 1 1/4" squares, gold
- Cut 28: 1 5/8" squares, gold
- Cut 28: 1 5/8" squares, light print
- Cut 84: 1 1/4" squares, light print
- Cut 60: 1 1/4" squares, dark
- Cut 20: 1 5/8" squares, dark
- Cut 58: 1 1/4" x 3 1/2" strips, dark
- Cut 3: 1 3/4" x 44" strips, dark, for the binding
- Cut 114: 1 1/4" squares, leaf print
- Cut 2: 1 3/4" x 20" strips, leaf print
- Cut 2: 1 3/4" x 28" strips, leaf print
- Cut 30: 1 1/4" squares, burgundy
- Cut 20: 1 5/8" squares, burgundy

DIRECTIONS
- Draw a diagonal line, corner to corner on the wrong side of each 1 5/8" light print square and each 1 5/8" burgundy square, as shown.
- Sandwich a 1 5/8" gold square with a 1 5/8" light print square, right sides together. Working with the gold and light print square as one unit, stitch 1/4" from each side of the drawn line. Repeat for all 28 gold/light print units.
- Cut the squares along the diagonal line. Each square yields 2 pieced squares.
- Clip the extra fabric caused by the seam. Press the squares open. You will have 56 gold and light print pieced squares.

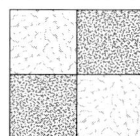

- Sandwich a 1 5/8" burgundy square and a 1 5/8" dark square, right sides together. Stitch 1/4" from the drawn diagonal line through both squares. Repeat for all 20 dark and burgundy squares.
- Cut the squares along the drawn diagonal line. Each square yields 2 pieced squares.
- Clip the extra fabric and press the squares open. You will have 40 dark and burgundy pieced squares.
- Stitch a 1 1/4" light print square and a 1 1/4" leaf print square together in pairs. Stitch 56 pairs.

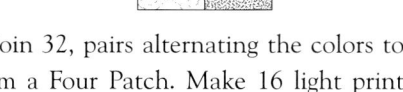

- Join 32, pairs alternating the colors to form a Four Patch. Make 16 light print and leaf print Four Patches.

Make 16

- Stitch a 1 1/4" dark square and a 1 1/4" leaf print square together in pairs. Stitch 40 pairs.
- Join 16 pairs alternating colors to form a Four Patch. Make 8 dark and leaf print Four Patches.

Make 8

- Stitch a light print and leaf print pair to a dark and leaf print pair. The leaf print should be in opposite corners of the Four Patch. Make 24.

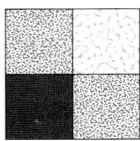

Make 24

- Lay out a 1 1/4" gold square, 2 gold and light print pieced squares and a 1 1/4" light print square in a Four Patch arrangement of 2 rows of 2, as shown.

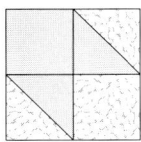

Make 28

- Stitch the squares into pairs. Join the pairs. Make 28 gold Four Patches.
- Lay out a 1 1/4" burgundy square, 2 burgundy and dark pieced squares and 1 1/4" dark square, as shown.

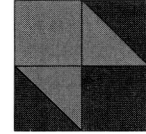

Make 20

- Join the squares into pairs. Join the pairs. Make 20 burgundy Four Patches.
- Lay out 2 gold Four Patches and 2 light print and leaf print Four Patches, as shown, in 2 rows of 2.

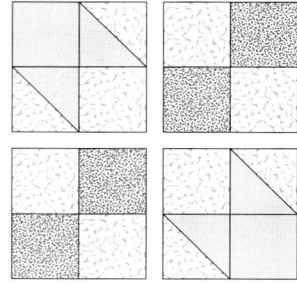

Block 1 Make 8

- Stitch the Four Patches in pairs. Join the pairs. Make 8 Block 1's.

- Lay out 2 burgundy Four Patches and 2 leaf print and dark Four Patches in 2 rows of 2.

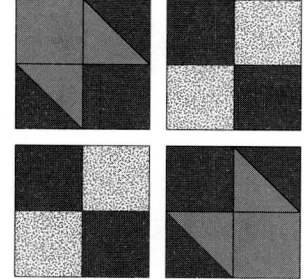

Corner Block Make 4

- Stitch the Four Patches in pairs. Join the pairs. Make 4 Corner Blocks.

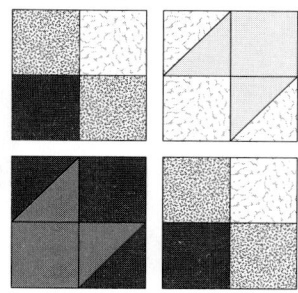

Block 2 Make 12

- Lay out a gold Four Patch, a burgundy Four Patch and 2 leaf print and light print and dark Four Patches, as shown.
- Stitch the Four Patches in pairs. Join the pairs. Make 12 Block 2's.
- Set the blocks aside.
- Referring to Row A in the Assembly Diagram, stitch a row of three 1 1/4" leaf print squares, two 1 1/4" burgundy squares and four 1 1/4" x 3 1/2" dark strips end to end in the following order: leaf print square, dark strip, burgundy square, dark strip, leaf print square, dark strip, burgundy square, dark strip, leaf print square. Make 2. Label them Row A.

Make additional rows as follows:
- **Row B (make 3)** burgundy square, dark strip, leaf print square, dark strip, gold square, dark strip, leaf print square, dark strip, burgundy square.
- **Row C (make 2)** leaf print square, dark strip, gold square, dark strip, leaf print square, dark strip, gold square, dark strip and leaf print square.
- Lay out the quilt following the Assembly Diagram for block and row placement. Place a 1 1/4" x 3 1/2" dark strip between each block and at the ends of each block row. Rotate the blocks as needed until the layout matches the Assembly Diagram and photo.
- Stitch the blocks and strips into rows. Join the rows.
- Stitch the 1 3/4" x 28" leaf print strips to the long sides of the quilt. Start and stop stitching 1/4" from the edge.
- Stitch the 1 3/4" x 20" leaf print strips to the remaining sides of the quilt. Start and stop stitching 1/4" from the edge.
- Refer to *Mini Stitching Tips* and miter each corner.
- Finish as described in *Mini Stitching Tips* using the 1 3/4" x 44" dark strips to form a continuous border.

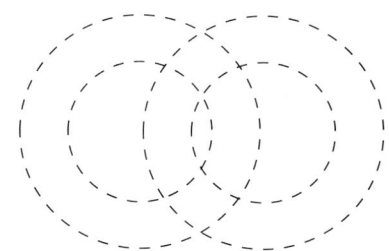

Assembly Diagram

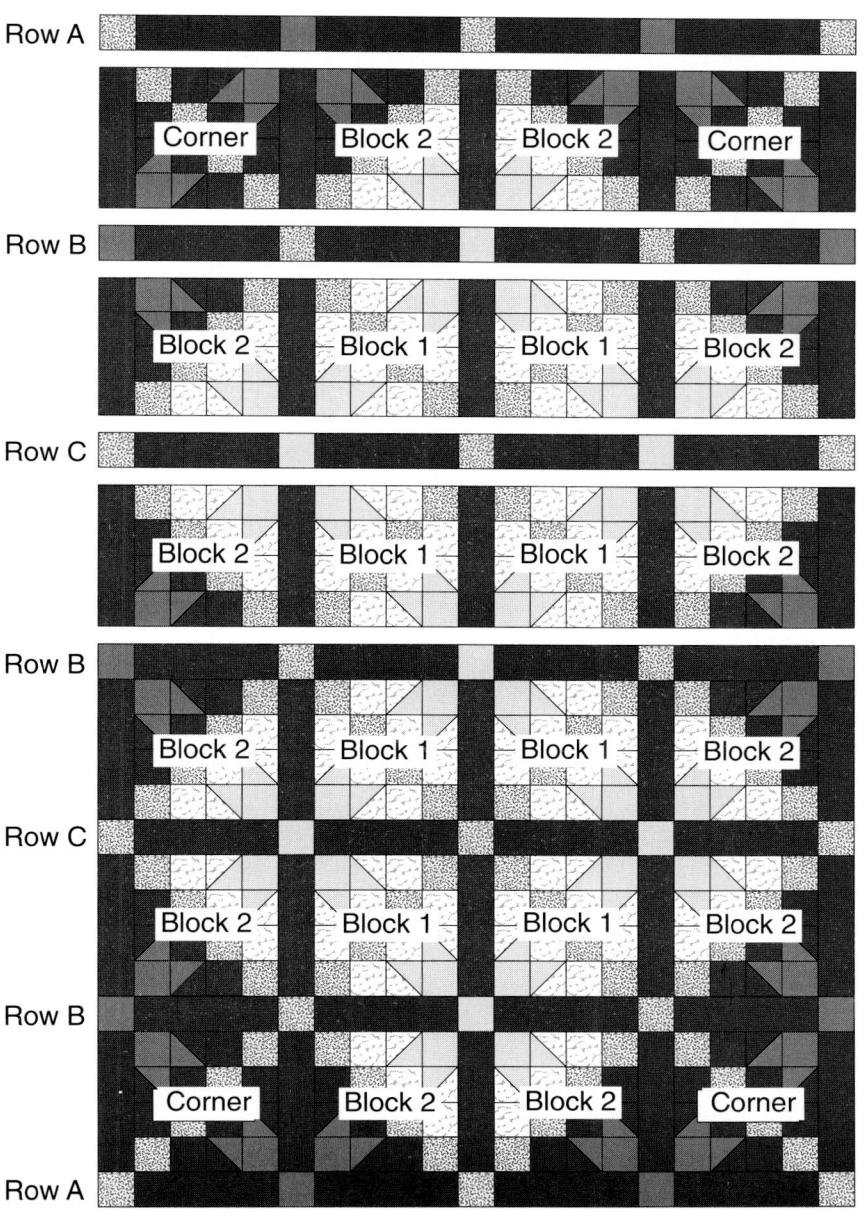

Embroidery Stitches

Outline Stitch

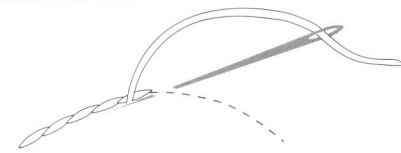

Running Stitch

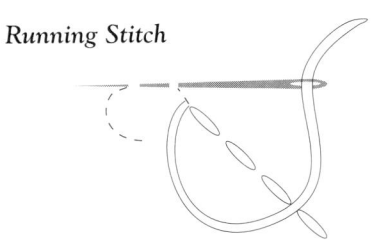

Lazy-Daisy Stitch

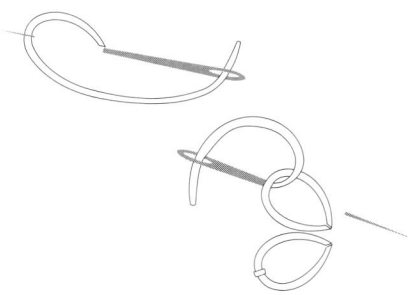

Cross-Stitch

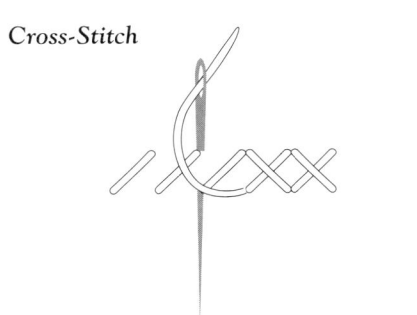

Herringbone Stitch

Chevron Stitch

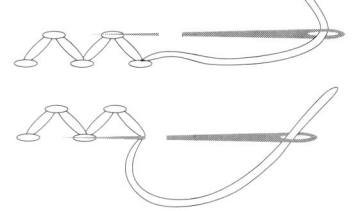

Shown on page 22

Silk Memories

Create memories to last a lifetime!

QUILT SIZE 9" x 10"

MATERIALS
- A skein of embroidery floss, in your favorite color
- Assortment of silk ties (opened and pressed) or scraps of silk fabric
- 9" x 10" piece of muslin
- 9" x 10" piece of backing fabric

CUTTING
- Scraps will be cut as they are added to the foundation; there is no need to pre-cut.

DIRECTIONS
- Lay the muslin foundation on a flat surface and draw a line 1" from each edge, as shown. This is the border stitching line.

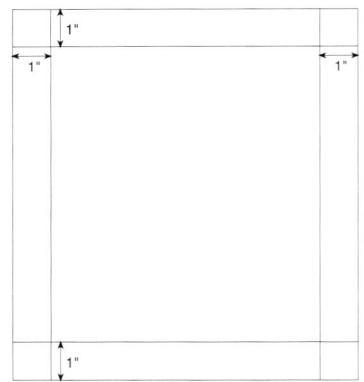

- The Foundation Diagram is for reference only. You may use pieces larger or smaller than those indicated.
- Solid lines represent stitching fabric directly to the foundation. Dotted lines show where fabric is stitched together, first, then sewn to the foundation in a row. Each seam must be covered by fabric in the next row or appliquéd in place on the foundation.
- Begin with a piece of fabric at position #1. Lay a second fabric right side against the first. Stitch through both fabrics and the foundation.
- Finger press the seam open.

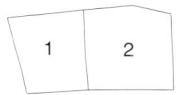

- Attach a 3rd fabric by placing a piece large enough to cover the 1-2 seam. Lay it right side against the 1st and 2nd pieces. Stitch through the foundation.
- Finger press the pieces open. Trim 3 to shape desired.

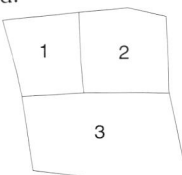

- Attach as many small scraps together as needed to cover fabric 1 and 3 at position 4. Stitch in place. Trim.

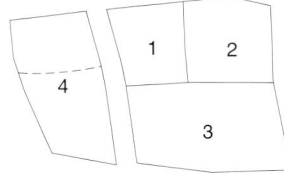

- Continue around the pattern until the quilt has extended past the 1" pencil lines on the foundation.
- Cut two 1 1/2" x 7 1/2" silk strips and stitch them to the short sides of the quilt.

Cretan Stitch

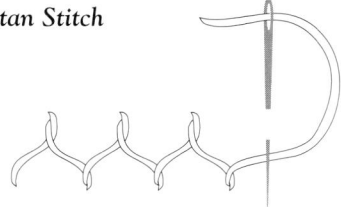

Feather Stitch

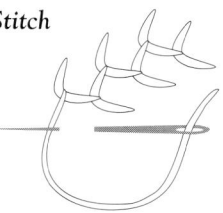

- Cut two 1 1/2" x 11" silk strips and stitch them to the remaining sides of the quilt.
- Refer to the embroidery stitches shown and embroider over all seams using embroidery stitches. Add any other embellishments you desire.
- Layer the back wrong side up/batting/and top right side up. Tie or tack the 3 layers together in several places to hold it securely.
- Bind using 1 3/4" silk fabric and the continuous binding method in *Mini Stitching Tips*.

Full-Size Foundation Diagram

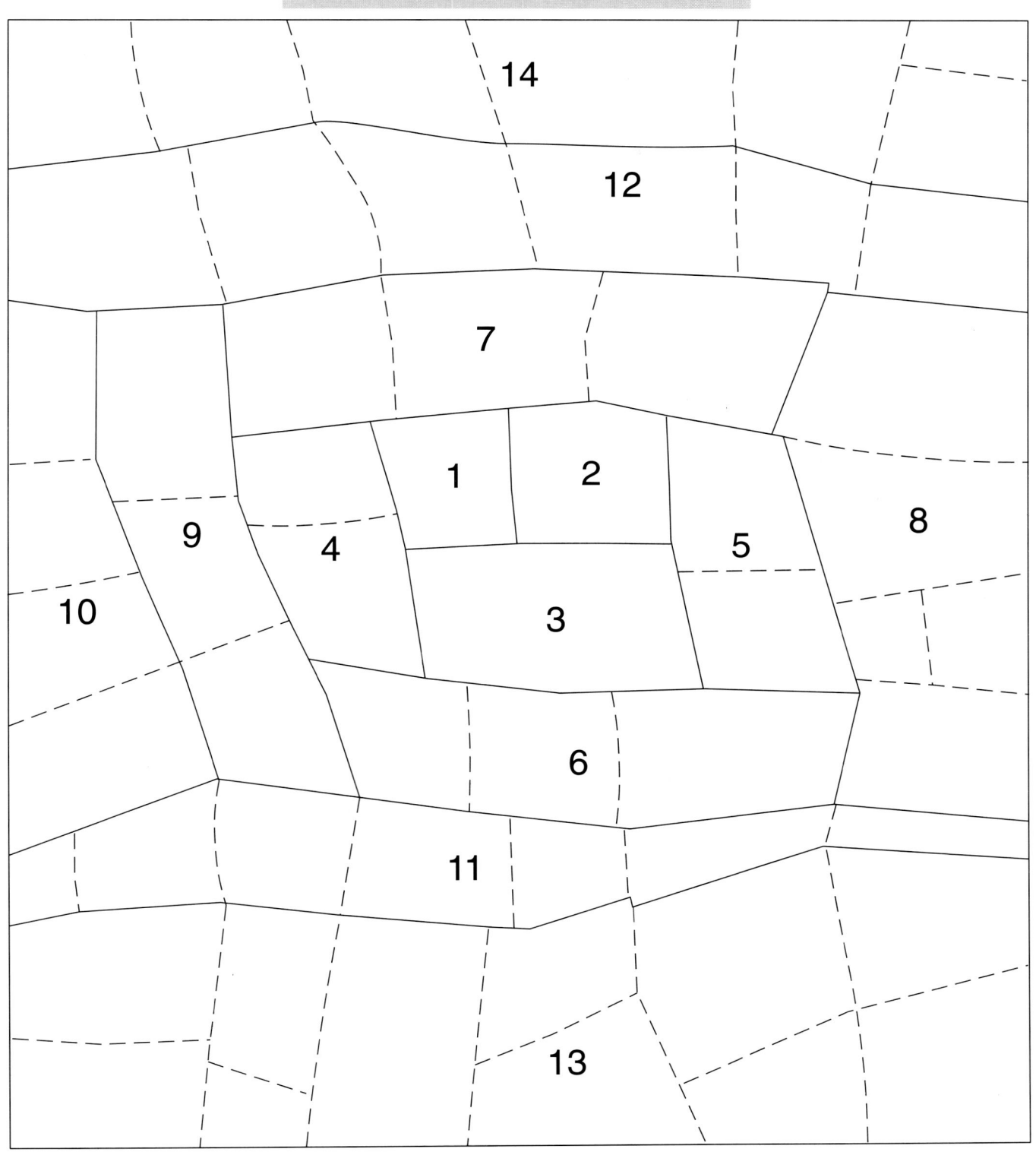

Windblown Lily

Shown on page 23

This Lily will warm you when the coldest winds blow!

QUILT SIZE 14" x 18 1/4"
BLOCK SIZE 3" square

MATERIALS

Yardage is estimated for 44" fabric.
- Quilter's quarter (18" x 22") of violet
- Quilter's quarter of green
- Quilter's quarter of muslin
- Quilter's quarter of light print
- Quilter's quarter of blue print
- 16" x 20" piece of backing fabric
- 16" x 20" piece of batting
- 2" square of clear template plastic

CUTTING

Dimensions include 1/4" seam allowance.
- Cut 6: A, violet, or cut three 1 3/8" squares in half diagonally
- Cut 6: B, violet
- Cut 6: C, violet, or cut three 2 3/8" squares in half diagonally
- Cut 2: 1" x 10 1/2" strips, violet
- Cut 2: 1" x 14 1/2" strips, violet
- Cut 6: 5/8" x 3" bias strips, green
- Cut 24: A, green, or cut twelve 1 3/8" squares in half diagonally
- Cut 12: D, green, or cut six 1 7/8" squares in half diagonally
- Cut 2: 3 1/2" squares, light print
- Cut 6: E, light print, or cut two 5 1/2" squares in quarters diagonally for the setting triangles
- Cut 4: F, light print, or cut two 3" squares in half diagonally for the corner triangles
- Cut 2: 2 1/2" x 18" strips, blue print
- Cut 2: 2 1/2" x 15" strips, blue print
- Cut 4: 1 3/4" x 22" strips, blue print for the binding
- Cut 54: A, muslin, or cut twenty-seven 1 3/8" squares in half diagonally
- Cut 12: D, muslin, or cut six 1 7/8" squares in half diagonally
- Cut 12: 1" x 2" rectangles, muslin
- Cut 6: 2" squares, muslin

DIRECTIONS

- Stitch a muslin A to each side of a violet A, as shown.

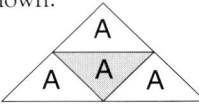

- Stitch a muslin A to the ends of a violet B, as shown.

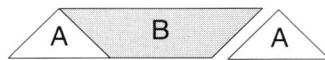

- Join the 2 pieced units. Make 6 buds.

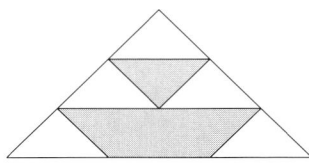

- Stitch a violet C to the buds to complete the flower square.

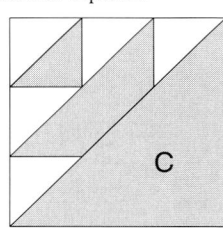

- Stitch a green A to a muslin A. Make 24 pieced squares.
- Stitch the pieced squares in pairs. Make 6 of each pair shown.

- Stitch a green D to a muslin D. Make 12 D squares.
- Stitch a pair of A squares to a D square, as shown. Join a 1" x 2" muslin rectangle to one side. Make six of each, exactly as shown, for the left and right leaf squares.

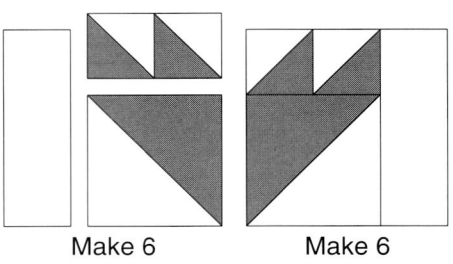

- Fold the 5/8" x 3" bias strip over 1/3 the width, wrong sides together, along the long side of the strip. Press to hold the fold.

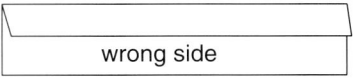

- Lay the 2" muslin square over the full-size pattern piece and trace the placement line for the stem on the muslin. Repeat for all six 2" muslin squares.
- Appliqué the folded edge of the green bias strip along the inside curve. Trim the seam to 1/8".
- Appliqué the outer edge of the curve by using your needle to fold the fabric under. Complete all 6 stem squares.
- Lay out a Lily Block using a stem square, a left and a right leaf square and the flower square.

- Join the squares into pairs. Join the pairs to complete the Lily Block. Make 6 Lily Blocks.

- Lay out the 6 Lily Blocks on point. Place the 3 1/2" light print squares between the blocks and the setting and corner triangles around the quilt.
- Stitch the quilt together in diagonal rows.
- Center and stitch a 1" x 10 1/2" violet strip to a 2 1/2" x 15" blue print strip. Make 2 pieced strips.
- Center, pin and stitch the pieced strips to the short sides of the quilt. Start and stop stitching 1/4" from the quilt edge.
- Center and stitch a 1" x 14 1/2" violet strip to a 2 1/2" x 18" blue strip. Make 2 pieced strips.
- Center, pin and stitch the pieced strips to the remaining sides of the quilt. Start and stop stitching 1/4" from the quilt edge.
- Refer to *Mini Stitching Tips* and miter each corner.
- Finish following the instructions in *Mini Stitching Tips*.

Quilting Design for Whole and Half Setting Blocks

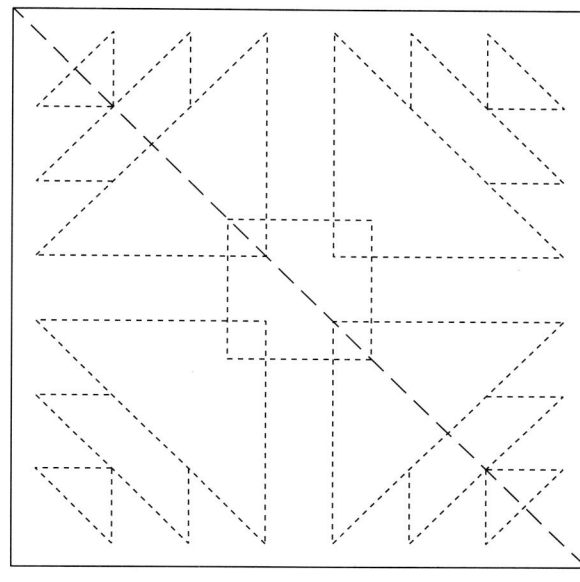

Full-Size Patterns for Windblown Lily

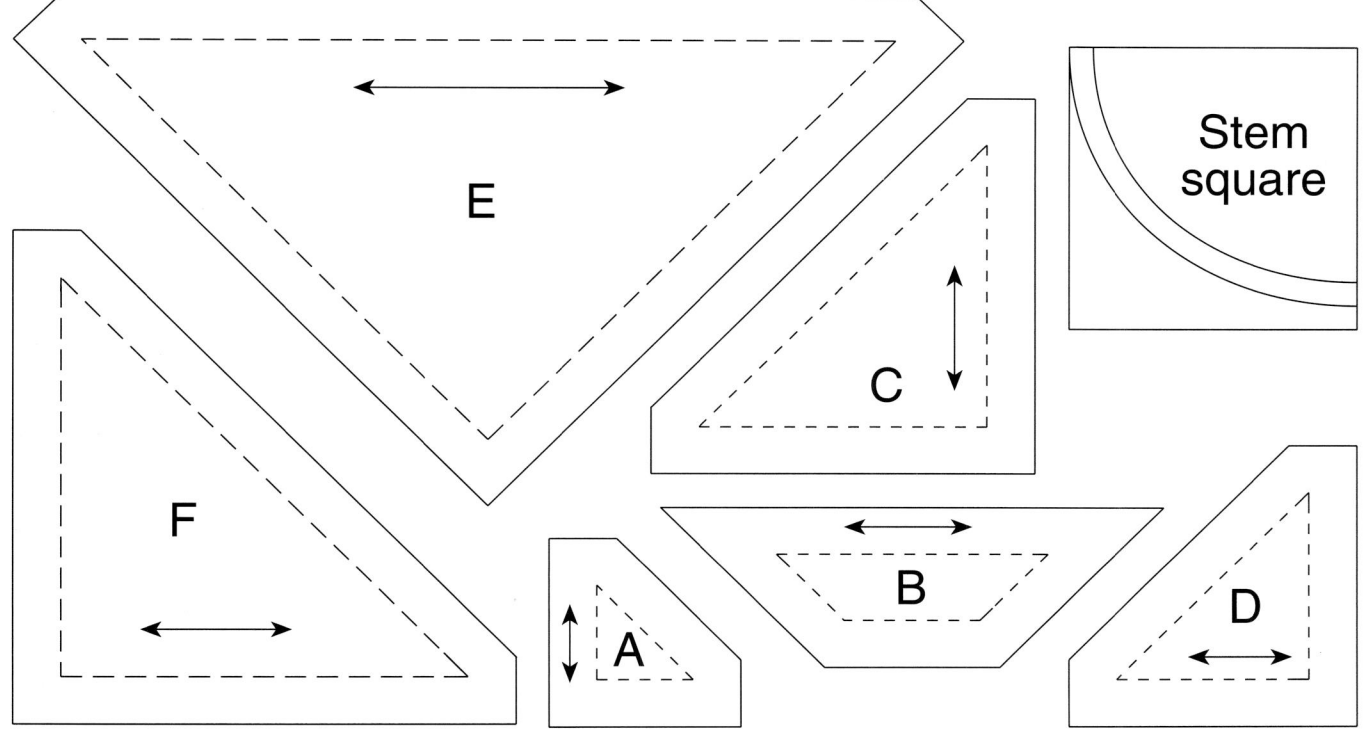

Magnolia

Strip piecing and templates for picture perfect flowers!

QUILT SIZE 19 1/4" x 23 1/2"
BLOCK SIZE 3" square

MATERIALS

Yardage is estimated for 44" fabric.
- 5/8 yard of cream for background and middle border
- 5/8 yard of green print for center square and bud base
- 5/8 yard of purple print for flower and binding
- 1/4 yard of purple for bud
- 1/8 yard of 2nd purple print for the inner border
- 1/8 yard of 2nd green print for the outer border
- 22" x 26" piece of backing fabric
- 22" x 26" piece of batting
- 5" square piece of template plastic

PREPARATION

- Trace pattern pieces A and B on clear template plastic. Transfer the line on the pattern piece to the templates with a permanent marker.
- Refer to *Mini Stitching Tips* for information on cutting bias strips. Begin with a 22" square.

CUTTING

Dimensions include 1/4" seam allowance.
- Cut 8: 1" x 20" bias strips, green print, for the bud base
- Cut 1: 1" x 15" strip, green print
- Cut 8: 1" x 20" bias strips, purple print, for the flower
- Cut 3: 1 3/4" x 44" strips, purple print, for the binding
- Cut 3: 1 1/2" x 44" strips, purple
- Cut 3: 1 1/2" x 44" strips, cream
- Cut 2: 1 3/4" x 15" strips, cream
- Cut 24: 1" x 1 3/4" rectangles, cream
- Cut 48: 1 1/8" squares, cream
- Cut 6: 3 1/2" squares, cream
- Cut 2: 3" squares, cream, cut in half diagonally for 4 corner triangles
- Cut 3: 5 1/2" squares, cream, cut in quarters diagonally—use 10 for setting triangles
- Cut 2: 1 1/4" x 15 3/4" strips, cream, for the middle border
- Cut 2: 1 1/4" x 18 1/2" strips, cream, for the middle border
- Cut 2: 1" x 14 1/4" strips, 2nd purple print, for the inner border
- Cut 2: 1" x 17 1/2" strips, 2nd purple print, for the inner border
- Cut 2: 2 1/4" x 19 1/4" strips, 2nd green print, for the outer border
- Cut 2: 2 1/4" x 20" strips, 2nd green print, for the outer border

DIRECTIONS

- Stitch a 1" x 20" green print bias strip to a 1" x 20" purple print bias strip right sides together along their length. Make 8 pieced bias strips.
- Lay template A on the pieced bias strip, aligning the fabric seam with the line on the template, as shown. Use only the A's that have the green print fabric in the tiny triangle. Set aside the other A's for another project.
- Trace around the template 6 times on each strip. Cut out the pieced triangles. You need 48 pieced triangles.
- Stitch a 1 1/2" x 44" purple strip to a 1 1/2" x 44" cream strip, right sides together, along their length. Press the seam toward the purple fabric. Make 3 pieced strips.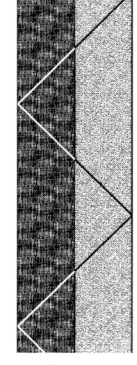
- Lay template B over a pieced strip, as shown. Trace around the template. Reverse the template and trace again. Trace a total of 32 triangles on each pieced strip. Cut out the pieced triangle. You need 48 B and 48 B reversed.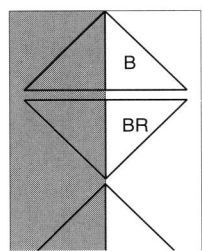
- Stitch a B and BR to adjacent sides of a 1 1/8" cream square, as shown. Place the purple half of the B triangles against the cream square. Make 48 Magnolia buds.

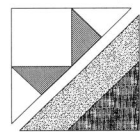

- Stitch the Magnolia buds to the A triangles, as shown. Make 48 Magnolias.
- Stitch a 1" x 15" green print strip between 1 3/4" x 15" cream strips. Press the seam away from the cream.
- Cut twelve 1" slices from the pieced strip.
- Lay out a block using 4 Magnolias, a 1" cream and green print slice and two 1" x 1 3/4" cream rectangles, as shown.

- Stitch a cream rectangle between 2

Magnolias to form a row.
- Stitch the cream/green print slice between Magnolia rows to form a block. Make 12 blocks.
- Lay the blocks on point in 4 rows of 3. Place the six 3 1/2" cream squares between the blocks. Place 10 cream setting triangles and 4 corner triangles around the quilt.

- Stitch the squares and triangles in diagonal rows. Join the rows.
- Stitch the 1" x 17 1/2" 2nd purple print strips to the long sides of the quilt.
- Stitch the 1" x 14 1/4" 2nd purple print strips to the remaining sides of the quilt.
- Stitch the 1 1/4" x 18 1/2" cream strips to the long sides and the 1 1/4" x 15 3/4" cream strips to the remaining sides of the quilt for the middle border.
- Stitch the 2 1/4" x 20" 2nd green print strips to the long sides and the 19 1/4" 2nd green print strips to the remaining sides.
- Finish according to *Mini Stitching Tips*. Make a continuous binding using the 1 3/4" purple print strips.

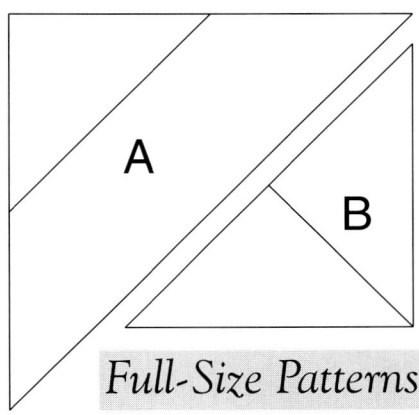

Full-Size Patterns

Stacked Bricks

Shown on page 21

Visit an old favorite!

QUILT SIZE 16" x 16 1/2"
BLOCK SIZE 3/4" x 2 3/4"

MATERIALS
Yardage is estimated for 44" fabric.
- Fabric scraps at least 1 1/4" x 3 1/4" in shades of purple
- 1/4 yard light for the background
- 1 yard border print for border and binding; if the print repeats fewer than 7 times, you'll need more fabric
- 18" x 19" piece of backing fabric
- 18" x 19" piece of batting

CUTTING
Dimensions include 1/4" seam allowance. Lengthwise strips are cut parallel to the selvage edge. Cut these first.
- Cut 3: 1 3/4" x 13 1/2" lengthwise strips, border print, centering the design
- Cut 4: 1 3/4" x 17 1/2" lengthwise strips, border print, centering the design
- Cut 2: 1 3/4" x 36" lengthwise strips, border print, for the binding
- Cut 56: 1 1/4" x 3 1/4" rectangles from scraps, for bricks
- Cut 112: 1 1/4" squares, light

DIRECTIONS
- Stitch a 1 1/4" light square to each end of a 1 1/4" x 3 1/4" scrap rectangle.

- Stitch 2 rows of 14 rectangles, offsetting each rectangle, as shown. For a scrappy look choose the rectangles at random.

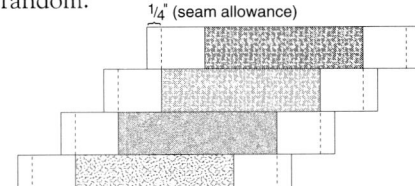

- Stitch 2 rows of 14 rectangles, offsetting each rectangle, as shown.

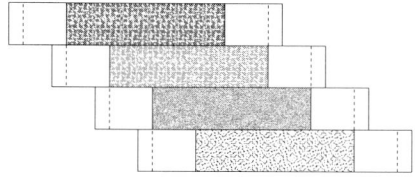

- Lay the rows one at a time on the cutting mat and trim 1/4" from the intersection of the rectangle and the end squares on both sides of each row.

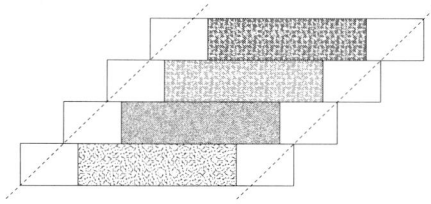

- Measure each row and square the ends at 13 1/2".
- Stitch a 1 3/4" x 13 1/2" border print strip between each of the 4 rows.

- Center and stitch a 1 3/4" x 17 1/2" border print strip to each side of the quilt. Start and stop stitching 1/4" from the quilt edge.
- Miter each corner referring to *Mini Stitching Tips*, as necessary.
- Finish as described in *Mini Stitching Tips*.

Raspberry Confetti

Interconnecting blocks add a special touch!

Shown on page 23

QUILT SIZE 23 1/2" square
BLOCK SIZE 4 1/2" square

MATERIALS
Yardage is estimated for 44" fabric.
- 3/4 yard purple print
- 1/4 yard red
- 1 yard light
- 25" square piece of backing fabric
- 25" square piece of batting
- 1" clear template plastic

PREPARATION
• Trace the 1" square template on clear plastic. Transfer the diagonal line exactly as shown. Cut out the template.

CUTTING
Dimensions include 1/4" seam allowance.
- Cut 9: 1" x 44" strips, purple print
- Cut 36: 2" squares, purple print
- Cut 1: 1" x 11" strip, purple print
- Cut 3: 1 3/4" x 44" strips, purple print, for the binding
- Cut 16: D, red
- Cut 128: C, red or cut sixty-four 1 3/8" squares in half diagonally
- Cut 9: 1" x 44" strips, light
- Cut 40: 1" squares, light
- Cut 2: 2 1/2" x 11" strips, light
- Cut 18: 1" x 2 1/2" rectangles, light
- Cut 64: C, light or cut thirty-two 1 3/8" squares in half diagonally
- Cut 24: F, light
- Cut 16: E, light or cut three 2 1/4" squares in quarters diagonally
- Cut 12: 1" x 5" strips, light
- Cut 4: 2" x 24" strips, light

DIRECTIONS
• Stitch a 1" x 44" light strip to a 1" x 44" purple print strip right sides together along their length. Make 9 pieced strips.

• Lay the 1" square template over the strip aligning the fabric seam with the diagonal line on the template. Trace around the template 24 times on each pieced strip. You will need a total of 216 pieced squares. If you prefer, use your square ruler and cut 1" squares with the ruler's 45° line along the fabric seamline.

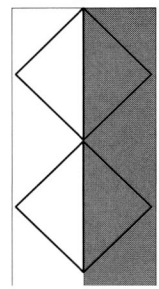

• Make 36 rows consisting of 3 pieced squares exactly as shown. Label them Row A.

 Row A

• Make 36 rows of 3 pieced squares, adding a 1" light square to one end exactly as shown. Label them row B.

Row B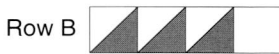

• Stitch an A and a B row to adjacent sides of a 2" purple print square. Make 36 Bear's Paw squares.

• Stitch a 1" x 11" purple print strip between 2 1/2" x 11" light strips.
• Cut nine 1" slices from the pieced strip.

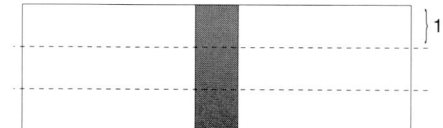

• Lay out a block using 4 Bear's Paw squares, a 1" purple and light slice and two 1" x 2 1/2" light rectangles, as shown.

• Stitch a 1" x 2 1/2" light rectangle between Bear's Paw squares to form a row.
• Stitch the 1 1/2" purple and light slice between the Bear's Paw rows. Make 9 Bear's Paw Blocks.
• Stitch a light C to opposite sides of a red D square. Stitch a light C to each remaining side of the red square. Make 16 C-D units.

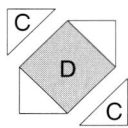

• Stitch 2 red C's to each end of F, as shown. Complete 24 C-F units this way.

• Refering to the row diagrams at right, lay out a Bear's Paw row using 4 C-F units and 3 Bear's Paw blocks. Stitch the C-F units to the Bear's Paws. Make 3 rows in this manner.
• Lay out a sashing row as shown in the Sashing row diagram at right, alternating 4 C-D squares and 3 C-F units. Stitch the C-F's to the C-D's end to end. Make 4

Sashing rows.
- Stitch the Bear's Paw rows between the Sashing rows.
- Stitch a red C to adjacent sides of a light E. Make 16.

- Make a Border row as shown in the diagram below, alternating 4 C-E's with three 1" x 5" light strips. Make 4 pieced rows in this manner.
- Stitch a pieced Border row to opposite sides of the quilt, completing the star design.
- Stitch a 1" light square to each end of the remaining pieced Border rows.
- Then stitch these rows to the remaining sides of the quilt.
- Stitch a 2" x 24" light strip to each side of quilt. Start and stop stitching 1/4" from the edge.
- Refer to *Mini Stitching Tips* and miter each corner.
- Finish following instructions in *Mini Stitching Tips* using the 1 3/4" purple print strips to make a continuous binding.

Full-Size Patterns for Raspberry Confetti

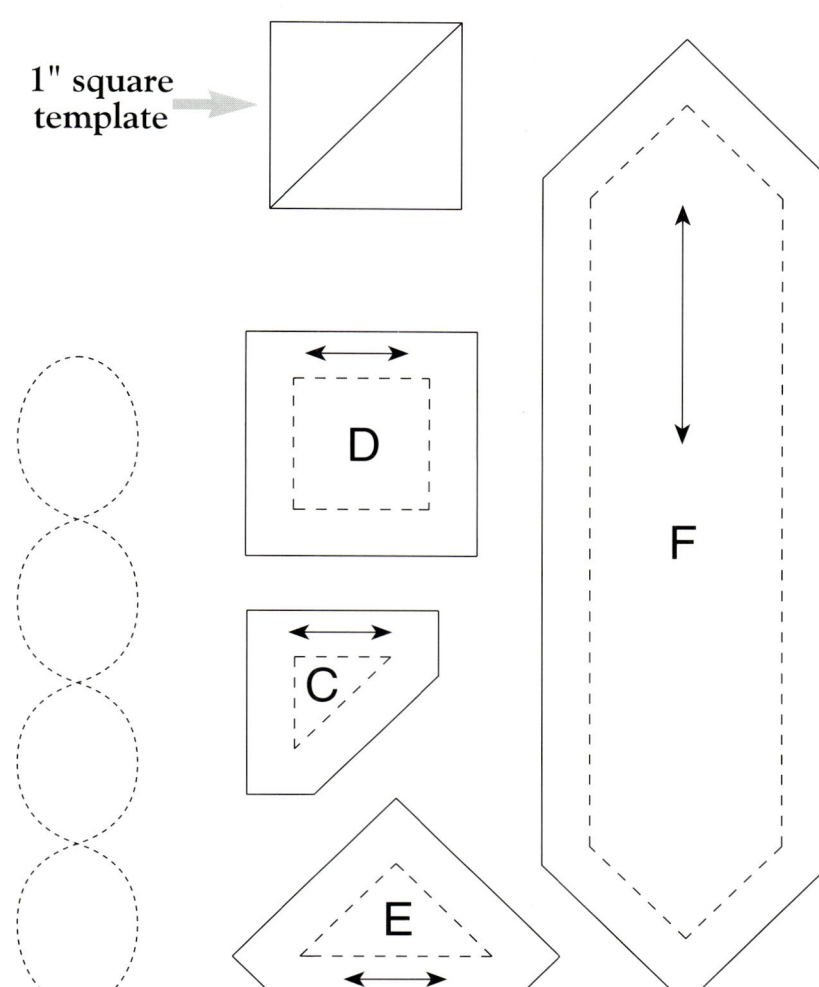

Quilting Design

Bear's Paw row - Make 3

Sashing row - Make 4

Border row - Make 4

39

ALSO BY CHITRA PUBLICATIONS

Magazines

Miniature Quilts
Quilting Today
Traditional Quiltworks

For subscription information, write to Chitra Publications,
2 Public Avenue, Montrose, PA 18801
or call 1-800-628-8244 (M-F, 8-4:30 EST)

Books

The Best of Miniature Quilts, Volume I compiled by Patti Lilik Bachelder

Tiny Amish Traditions by Sylvia Trygg Voudrie

Tiny Traditions by Sylvia Trygg Voudrie

Designing New Traditions in Quilts by Sharyn Squier Craig

Drafting Plus: 5 Simple Steps to Pattern Drafting and More! by Sharyn Squier Craig

Quilting Design Treasury by Anne Szalavary

Small Folk Quilters by Ingrid Rogler

A Stitcher's Christmas Album by Patti Lilik Bachelder

Theorem Appliqué: Book 1, Abundant Harvest by Patricia B. Campbell and Mimi Ayars

Theorem Appliqué: Book 2, Summer Splendor by Patricia B. Campbell and Mimi Ayars

Quilts from Grandma's Attic by Chitra Publications, Edited by Kent Ward